ECONOMIC ISSUES, PROBLEMS AND PERSPECTIVES

# OCCUPATIONAL LICENSING

# BENEFITS, COSTS, AND ISSUES

# ECONOMIC ISSUES, PROBLEMS AND PERSPECTIVES

Additional books in this series can be found on Nova's website under the Series tab.

Additional e-books in this series can be found on Nova's website under the e-book tab.

ECONOMIC ISSUES, PROBLEMS AND PERSPECTIVES

# OCCUPATIONAL LICENSING

# BENEFITS, COSTS, AND ISSUES

MARGIE CASTRO
EDITOR

nova publishers
*New York*

**Library of Congress Cataloging-in-Publication Data**

ISBN: 978-1-63484-340-9

*Published by Nova Science Publishers, Inc. † New York*

# CONTENTS

# PREFACE

Over the past several decades, the share of U.S. workers holding an occupational license has grown sharply. When designed and implemented carefully, licensing can offer important health and safety protections to consumers, as well as benefits to workers. However, the current licensing regime in the United States also creates substantial costs, and often the requirements for obtaining a license are not in sync with the skills needed for the job. There is evidence that licensing requirements raise the price of goods and services, restrict employment opportunities, and make it more difficult for workers to take their skills across State lines. Too often, policymakers do not carefully weigh these costs and benefits when making decisions about whether or how to regulate a profession through licensing. In some cases, alternative forms of occupational regulation, such as State certification, may offer a better balance between consumer protections and flexibility for workers. This book outlines the growth of licensing over the past several decades, its costs and benefits, and its impacts on workers and work arrangements. The book recommends several best practices to ensure that licensing protects consumers without placing unnecessary restrictions on employment, innovation, or access to important goods and services.

In: Occupational Licensing
Editor: Margie Castro
ISBN: 978-1-63484-340-9


*Chapter 1*

# OCCUPATIONAL LICENSING: A FRAMEWORK FOR POLICYMAKERS*

***Department of the Treasury Office of Economic Policy, the Council of Economic Advisers, and the Department of Labor***

## EXECUTIVE SUMMARY

Over the past several decades, the share of U.S. workers holding an occupational license has grown sharply. When designed and implemented carefully, licensing can offer important health and safety protections to consumers, as well as benefits to workers. However, the current licensing regime in the United States also creates substantial costs, and often the requirements for obtaining a license are not in sync with the skills needed for the job. There is evidence that licensing requirements raise the price of goods and services, restrict employment opportunities, and make it more difficult for workers to take their skills across State lines. Too often, policymakers do not carefully weigh these costs and benefits when making decisions about whether or how to regulate a profession through licensing. In some cases, alternative forms of occupational regulation, such as State certification, may offer a better balance between consumer protections and flexibility for workers.

* This is an edited, reformatted and augmented version of a report issued by the Council of Economic Advisers, July 2015.

This report outlines the growth of licensing over the past several decades, its costs and benefits, and its impacts on workers and work arrangements. The report recommends several best practices to ensure that licensing protects consumers without placing unnecessary restrictions on employment, innovation, or access to important goods and services.

**Occupational licensing has grown rapidly over the past few decades.**

- More than one-quarter of U.S. workers now require a license to do their jobs, with most of these workers licensed by the States. The share of workers licensed at the State level has risen five-fold since the 1950s.
- About two-thirds of this change stems from an increase in the number of professions that require a license, with the remaining growth coming from changing composition of the workforce.

**When designed and implemented carefully, licensing can benefit consumers through higher-quality services and improved health and safety standards.**

- In some cases, licensing helps to ensure high-quality services, safeguard against serious harms, and offer workers clear guidelines around professional development and training.
- However, to realize these benefits licensing requirements must closely match the qualifications needed to perform the job, a goal that is not always achieved or may not be maintained when licensing expands and jobs change.
- Licensing may also help practitioners to professionalize, encouraging individuals to invest in occupational skills and creating career paths for licensed workers. For example, accountants in States requiring more experience (three or more years) are 26 to 36 percent more likely to have acquired training since starting their current job.

**But by making it harder to enter a profession, licensing can also reduce employment opportunities and lower wages for excluded workers, and increase costs for consumers.**

- Research shows that by imposing additional requirements on people seeking to enter licensed professions, licensing can reduce total employment in the licensed professions.
- Estimates find that unlicensed workers earn 10 to 15 percent lower wages than licensed workers with similar levels of education, training, and experience.
- Licensing laws also lead to higher prices for goods and services, with research showing effects on prices of between 3 and 16 percent. Moreover, in a number of other studies, licensing did not increase the quality of goods and services, suggesting that consumers are sometimes paying higher prices without getting improved goods or services.

**Licensing requirements vary substantially by State, creating barriers to workers moving across State lines and inefficiencies for businesses and the economy as a whole.**

- Estimates suggest that over 1,100 occupations are regulated in at least one State, but fewer than 60 are regulated in all 50 States, showing substantial differences in which occupations States choose to regulate. For example, funeral attendants are licensed in nine States and florists are licensed in only one State.
- The share of licensed workers varies widely State-by-State, ranging from a low of 12 percent in South Carolina to a high of 33 percent in Iowa. Most of these State differences are due to State policies, not differences in occupation mix across States.
- States also have very different requirements for obtaining a license. For example, Michigan requires three years of education and training to become a licensed security guard, while most other States require only 11 days or less. South Dakota, Iowa, and Nebraska require 16 months of education to become a licensed cosmetologist, while New York and Massachusetts require less than 8 months.
- Licensed workers are sometimes unable to use distance or online education to fulfill continuing education requirements, as some States do not automatically accept accreditation from good schools based in other States. Similarly, State licensing requirements can prevent workers from teleworking or taking advantage of new technologies, thereby inhibiting innovation.

**The costs of licensing fall disproportionately on certain populations.**

- About 35 percent of military spouses in the labor force work in professions that require State licenses or certification, and they are ten times more likely to have moved across State lines in the last year than their civilian counterparts. These military spouses may have difficulty acquiring a new license each time they move or meeting different license requirements in their new State.
- Licensing requirements often make it difficult for immigrants to work in fields where they have valuable experience and training. This deprives the U.S. market of a large share of their skills, and makes it difficult for these workers to make their full contribution to the workforce.
- In half the States, applicants can be denied a license due to any kind of criminal conviction, regardless of whether it is relevant to the license sought or how long ago it occurred. It often takes six months to a year for some States to simply review an applicant's criminal history and make an initial determination about whether she qualifies for a license.

**Best practices in licensing can allow States, working together or individually, to safeguard the well-being of consumers while maintaining a modernized regulatory system that meets the needs of workers and businesses. Licensing best practices include:**

- Limiting licensing requirements to those that address legitimate public health and safety concerns to ease the burden of licensing on workers.
- Applying the results of comprehensive cost-benefit assessments of licensing laws to reduce the number of unnecessary or overly-restrictive licenses.
- Within groups of States, harmonizing regulatory requirements as much as possible, and where appropriate entering into inter-State compacts that recognize licenses from other States to increase the mobility of skilled workers.
- Allowing practitioners to offer services to the full extent of their current competency, to ensure that all qualified workers are able to offer services.

In order for the economy to successfully continue to innovate and grow, we must ensure that we are able to take full advantage of all of America's talented labor. By one estimate, licensing restrictions cost millions of jobs nationwide and raise consumer expenses by over one hundred billion dollars. The stakes involved are high, and to help our economy grow to its full potential we need to create a 21st century regulatory system—one that protects public health and welfare while promoting economic growth, innovation, competition, and job creation.

## INTRODUCTION: WHY DOES OCCUPATIONAL LICENSING MATTER?

While the U.S. economy has grown substantially over the past 20 years, many American workers and their families have not fully shared in this growth.[1] To build on the Administration's progress in creating a stronger foundation for shared and sustainable growth, we must ensure that regulatory policies are designed appropriately to both expand economic opportunity and maintain the high performance of America's workers. President Obama in 2011 furthered these goals by signing an Executive Order ordering federal agencies to identify and use the "best, most innovative, and least burdensome tools for achieving regulatory ends," and outlining a number of steps agencies must take when regulating, such as using cost-benefit analysis and specifying performance objectives.[2]

Occupational licensing, a form of regulation that requires individuals who want to perform certain types of work to obtain the permission of the government, is also central to these goals. In many fields, occupational licensing plays an important role in protecting consumers and ensuring quality. Few people, for example, would feel comfortable traveling in a commercial plane flown by an unlicensed pilot or having a medical procedure performed by an unlicensed physician. However, licensing policies can be designed in many different ways, and the ways in which they are designed and implemented affect workers' access to jobs, the wages they are paid, the ease with which they can move across State lines, as well as consumers' access to essential goods and services. These factors in turn help determine dynamism and growth in the economy overall. This report examines the key issues surrounding occupational licensing, and identifies several ideas for optimizing licensing policy to meet the needs of today's economy.

Consumers are likely most familiar with licensing requirements for professionals like dentists, lawyers, and physicians, but today licensing requirements extend to a very broad set of workers. For example, florists, auctioneers, scrap metal recyclers, and barbers are all licensed in some States. Individuals working in a licensed occupation without a license can be forced to cease working, fined, or in some cases, even prosecuted and incarcerated. Licenses are most commonly issued and regulated by state governments, but localities and the Federal government also license certain forms of work. In total, about 25 percent of today's U.S. workforce is in an occupation licensed at the State level, up from less than 5 percent in the early 1950s, and this share is higher when local and Federal licenses are included.[3] This means that a large share of American jobs are only accessible to those with the time and means to complete what are often lengthy licensing requirements. One study found that for a subset of low- and medium-skilled jobs, the average license required around 9 months of education and training.[4]

There are few sources of comprehensive data on licensing in the United States, but the existing data show that licensing is widespread and that it varies substantially across States. According to the most recent estimates from the Council of State Governments, over 1,100 jobs were licensed, certified, or registered in at least one State. Of this number, fewer than 60 were regulated by all the States.[5,6] More recent evidence shows that States vary dramatically in their rates of licensure and training required to receive a license, suggesting that States are not treating occupations equivalently with regard to whether they do or do not require a license.[7]

When designed and implemented appropriately, licensing can benefit practitioners and consumers through improving quality and protecting public health and safety. This can be especially important in situations where it is costly or difficult for consumers to obtain information on service quality, or where low-quality practitioners can potentially inflict serious harm on consumers or the public at large. Doctors' competence, for instance, is difficult for their prospective patients to evaluate, and the consequences of inferior work may be severe. Licensing can also provide recourse for consumers when practitioners fail to safely or adequately deliver services. In addition, licensing can benefit practitioners by encouraging individuals to invest in lifelong occupational skills, thereby creating career paths for licensed workers.

Yet while licensing can bring benefits, current systems of licensure can also place burdens on workers, employers, and consumers, and too often are inconsistent, inefficient, and arbitrary. The evidence in this report suggests that licensing restricts mobility across States, increases the cost of goods and services to consumers, and reduces access to jobs in licensed occupations. The employment barriers created by licensing may raise wages for those who are successful in gaining entry to a licensed occupation, but they also raise prices for consumers and limit opportunity for other workers in terms of both wages and employment. By one estimate, licensing restrictions cost millions of jobs nationwide and raise consumer expenses by over one hundred billion dollars.[8] The barriers imposed by licensing can prevent workers from succeeding in the best job for them, which in turn makes our labor market less efficient and ultimately can limit economic growth.

These impacts may be especially harmful for certain populations. For example, military spouses, who are highly mobile and frequently have to relocate across State lines, have a difficult time obtaining a new license each time they move. Our licensure system can also prevent immigrants who have considerable training and work experience abroad from applying their skills in the U.S., since often they do not meet the relevant licensing requirements. In addition, licensing laws often contain blanket exclusions for the formerly incarcerated or those with criminal records, regardless of whether their records are relevant to the job for which they are applying. This renders a great number of individuals – as many as one in three Americans has some form of criminal record (either for an arrest or a conviction) – ineligible for a large share of jobs, in turn perpetuating unstable economic situations for these individuals.[9]

Licensing practices also need to keep pace with developments in today's economy. Current licensing requirements complicate the use of distance learning, which may rely on out-of-State providers, for both students and workers engaging in continuing education required in their fields. Moreover, students seeking to invest in training for a new career may not be aware of the full extent of license requirements or of how these vary across States and therefore limit their ability to relocate in the future. Licensing laws also frequently do not allow providers to offer services to the full extent of their competency, and may impede access to services in areas such as law and health care.

The relative magnitude of these costs and benefits depends on the specific circumstances for each profession, so licensing proposals being considered must be carefully weighed in each instance.[10] Important considerations include the risk posed to the public by unlicensed practitioners, the extent to which licensing requirements lead to quality improvements, and the impacts of licensing on the cost of goods and services, practitioner supply, and mobility. In some cases where public health and safety concerns are less salient, alternative forms of occupational regulation may be appropriate. For example, State certification requirements may restrict the use of a profession's title to those who have been certified, but allows anyone to perform the duties of the profession. In doing so, certification can provide consumers with additional information regarding providers' quality, without restricting consumer choice or limiting entry into the workforce.

## STREAMLINING LICENSING AND CREDENTIALING FOR SERVICE MEMBERS, VETERANS, AND MILITARY FAMILIES

Occupational licensing primarily falls to States, and to better serve our returning service members and their families, nearly all States have recently taken steps to ease the heavy burdens that our licensing system places on service members, veterans, and military families. Many jobs, like paramedics, truck drivers, nurses, and welders, require either a State occupational license or a national certification to be hired, and our current system of occupational regulation makes it very difficult for service members and veterans to obtain civilian licenses and certifications that directly translate to their military training. Oftentimes, service members and veterans are required to repeat education or training in order to receive these occupational credentials, even though much or all of their military training and experience overlaps with licensure or certification requirements. According to a 2012 survey, 60 percent of veteran respondents said they had trouble translating their military skills into civilian job experience.[a]

Furthermore, our patchwork system of State licensure creates additional challenges for military families, who are much more mobile than the general population and frequently have to acquire new licenses when they move across State lines. According to a joint analysis by the Department of Defense and the Department of the Treasury, about 35 percent of military spouses in the labor force work in professions that require State licenses or certification, and they are ten times more likely to have moved across State lines in the last year than their civilian counterparts.[b]

In response to these challenges, under the President's direction, the Department of Defense established the Military Credentialing and Licensing Task Force in 2012, charged with identifying and creating opportunities for service members to earn civilian occupational credentials and licenses through partnerships with national certifying bodies. With the help of the Task Force's efforts, hundreds of service members have earned or are in the process of earning machinist, logistics, welding, and engineering certifications for high-demand manufacturing jobs, and efforts are underway to develop similar pathways for the attainment of information technology certifications.

In addition, the Obama Administration has partnered with States to streamline State occupational licensing for service members, veterans, and their spouses. At the National Governors Association meeting in February 2012, First Lady Michelle Obama and Dr. Jill Biden called upon all 50 governors to help expedite professional licenses or certification for military spouses when they move to a new State. Through collaboration with State legislators and regulators, the Department of Defense has worked towards State adoption of best practices that can expedite the transfer of military spouse licenses that are in good standing and are substantially equivalent. [c] As of May 2015, all 50 States had streamlined the process for spousal licensing since First Lady Michelle Obama and Dr. Jill Biden's call to governors.[d]

[a] Iraq and Afghanistan Veterans of America and Prudential Financial, Inc. 2012. Veterans' Employment Challenges: Perceptions and Experiences of Transitioning from Military to Civilian Life. http:// www.prudential.com/ documents/ public/ VeteransEmployment Challenges.pdf.

[b] U.S. Department of the Treasury and U.S. Department of Defense. 2012. Supporting our Military Families: Best Practices for Streamlining Occupational Licensing Across State Lines. http://www.defense.gov/home/pdf/Occupational_Licensing_and_Military_ Spouses_Report_vFINAL.PDF.

[c] National Economic Council and Council of Economic Advisers. 2013. *The Fast Track to Civilian Employment: Streamlining Credentialing and Licensing for Service Members, Veterans, and their Spouses.*

[d] Department of Defense and States, Partnering to Support Military Families. "Removing Licensure Impediments for Transitioning Military Spouses." http://ww.usa4militaryfamilies.dod.mil/MOS/f?p=USA4:ISSUE:0:::: P2_ISSUE:2.

This report reviews the evidence on these costs and benefits, and examines the trends and State differences in licensing. There is ample evidence that States and other jurisdictions should review current licensing practices with an aim toward rationalizing these regulations and lowering barriers to employment. Toward this end, the final portion of this report provides guidance in the form of suggested best practices; an overview of various initiatives to alleviate the negative impacts of licensing, while still ensuring quality and protecting consumers; and a set of resources for policymakers seeking to take further action.

# I. The Costs and Benefits of Licensing

The key question for regulators, legislators, and the public is: do the benefits of current licensing requirements outweigh the costs? The answer will not be the same in every State and every occupation, but to begin to understand the tradeoffs, we first provide an overview of the major costs and benefits of licensing. We then provide a summary of the empirical research into whether these costs and benefits materialize.

## Benefits of Licensing

Licensing is usually justified on the grounds that it improves quality and protects the public against incompetent or dangerous practitioners. This argument is strongest when low-quality practitioners can potentially inflict serious harm, or when it is difficult for consumers to evaluate provider quality beforehand. This can be the case when, for example, it is difficult to learn a provider's reputation or to try out different providers, or when evaluation requires specialized knowledge or expertise.

Practitioners may also seek to become licensed as part of a move toward greater professionalization. Licensing represents the State's sanction of practitioners' work, and so licensing an occupation can confer legitimacy and increase social status for practitioners. It can also build community and cohesiveness within an occupation, and help to standardize work functions. When licensing functions in these ways, it can provide benefits to practitioners through increased recognition of their work and influence.[11]

Even when health and safety are not an issue, increasing consumer information through regulation can be beneficial. If consumers are unable to distinguish between high- and low- quality providers before purchasing a good or receiving a service, low-quality providers can remain in the market without being recognized as such, reducing the average quality in the market and reducing the incentives for other providers to invest in quality improvements.[12]

Furthermore, if consumers are sufficiently concerned about getting a low-quality provider, then informational uncertainty may depress demand for goods and services. Consumers who would otherwise purchase a product if they knew it were high-quality might forgo their purchase if the quality were uncertain. Licensing is one possible way to address these problems through forcing providers to meet certain quality benchmarks, and creating greater incentives to invest in increased training and skill development.

## Costs of Licensing

However, the quality, health and safety benefits of licensing do not always materialize. When they do, they come at a cost that is easy to overlook because it is borne by many different people and is difficult to observe in day-to-day experience.

First, by imposing requirements on people seeking to enter licensed professions—such as additional training and education, fees, exams, and paperwork—licensing reduces employment in the licensed occupation and hence competition, driving up the price of goods and services for consumers. This could benefit licensed practitioners, who might earn more than they would in an unlicensed market, or the financial benefits could flow elsewhere, such as to educational institutions or other licensing entities.[13] But the wages of workers who are excluded from the occupation are reduced in two ways. First, those who would otherwise have worked in a more highly paid occupation may enter a less well-paid occupation. Second, wages in less well-paid, unlicensed occupations may fall even lower due to the increased number of workers entering them. Lower wages in turn discourage labor force participation among the excluded, lowering their employment rate.

Through both of these channels, licensing can shift resources from workers with lower-income and fewer skills to those with higher income and skills. Data show that 52 percent of licensed workers hold a Bachelor's degree, compared to 38 percent of unlicensed workers.[14] Lower- income workers are less likely to be able to afford the tuition and lost wages associated with licensing's educational requirements, closing the door to many licensed jobs for them. It is also lower-income workers who are hurt if wages fall in unlicensed jobs, since on average, unlicensed workers earn 28 percent less than licensed workers.[15]

Fundamentally, licensing affects who takes what job. If licensing places too many restrictions on this allocation of workers, it can reduce the overall efficiency of the labor market. When workers cannot enter jobs that make the best use of their skills, this hampers growth and may even lessen innovation. Licensing may also affect entrepreneurship.[16] Licensed workers are more likely to be self-employed than other workers. Sixteen percent of licensed workers report being self- employed, as compared to 13 percent of unlicensed workers.[17] Just as important, entrepreneurs in new areas that overlap with a licensed occupation – such as someone who is creating a website to enable consumers to take legal action – may find themselves required to hold a license because a small part of their work overlaps with that of another licensed occupation. In this case, the web entrepreneur may be required to hold a law license.[18]

Finally, since many occupations are licensed at the State level, licensed practitioners typically have to acquire a new license when they move across States. This alone entails various procedural hurdles, such as paying fees, filling out administrative paperwork, and submitting an application and waiting for it to be processed. Moreover, since each State sets its own licensing requirements, these often vary across State lines, and licensed individuals seeking to move to another State often discover that they must meet new qualifications (such as education, experience, training, testing, etc.) if they want to continue working in their occupation. The resulting costs in both time and money can discourage people from moving or lead them to exit their occupation. This system is especially burdensome for some populations, such as military spouses, who are very likely to move across State lines.[19] Diminished mobility generates inefficiency in the labor market, with workers unable to migrate easily to the jobs in which they are most productive. In times of economic distress, this reduced mobility would be especially harmful, as workers would have a difficult time leaving – or for some practitioners, delivering services to – hard-hit areas.

## The Evidence on Licensing's Costs and Benefits

Empirical research on the costs and benefits of licensing stretches back several decades and focuses on a diverse set of occupations. We provide more detail on these studies in the Research Appendix, but here we summarize research on four major areas of licensing's impacts: service quality, prices, wages and employment, and worker mobility.

If licensing were able to limit the practice of an occupation to high-quality practitioners, then it would be expected to improve quality and public health and safety. A wide range of studies have examined whether this happens. With the caveats that the literature focuses on specific examples and that quality is difficult to measure, most research does not find that licensing improves quality or public health and safety. We summarize several studies on licensing's quality impacts in Research Appendix Table 1. Stricter licensing was associated with quality improvements in only 2 out of the 12 studies reviewed. There is also evidence that many licensing boards are not diligent in monitoring licensed practitioners, which contributes to a lack of quality improvement under licensing. These boards often rely on consumer complaints and third-party reports to monitor practitioner quality, but only a small fraction of consumer complaints result in any kind of disciplinary action.[20]

Quality can be defined in many ways and is often difficult to measure, but the evidence on licensing's effects on prices is unequivocal: many studies find that more restrictive licensing laws lead to higher prices for consumers. In 9 of the 11 studies we reviewed (see Research Appendix Table 2), significantly higher prices accompanied stricter licensing. To take just two examples, more restrictive State licensing of nurse practitioners raises the price of a well-child medical exam by 3 to 16 percent,[21] and imposing greater licensing requirements on dental hygienists and assistants increases the average price of a dental visit by 7 to 11 percent.[22]

While there is compelling evidence that licensing raises prices for consumers, there is less evidence on whether licensing restricts supply of occupational practitioners, which would be one way in which it might contribute to higher prices. This should appear as lower employment in licensed professions, relative to the employment that would prevail with less restricted entry. In one notable empirical study of the employment effects of licensing, researchers found that 100 additional hours of required training decreased the number of Vietnamese manicurists by almost 18 percent in a State.[23] This suggests that at least among licensed workers who face a choice of States in which to locate, more stringent licensing makes it less likely that workers will enter licensed professions in those States.

However, the effect of restricting entry to licensed occupations has generally proved easier to study in terms of wages: restrictions are expected to raise the wages of those who manage to enter licensed occupations, and lower the wages of other workers, leading to a wage gap.[24] Data from Kleiner and

Krueger (2013) show that, on average, licensed workers earn 28 percent more than unlicensed workers.[25] This gap in part reflects other differences between these two groups of workers that can contribute to higher earnings for licensed workers. It is therefore important to distinguish between licensed workers' wages rising due to artificial scarcity and rising due to the increased education and training brought about by licensing. Researchers have taken a number of approaches to account for these differences and get a better estimate of the true impact of licensing on wages. Estimates that account for differences in education, training, and experience find that licensing results in 10 percent to 15 percent higher wages for licensed workers relative to unlicensed workers.[26]

More sophisticated analyses seek to identify truly comparable groups of workers who differ only in terms of their licensure status. One approach is to compare workers in the same occupation but with different licensing status. This can happen because some States license an occupation while others do not, and also because States commonly only require some practitioners of an occupation to hold a license. A second approach is to compare earnings for the same workers as they switch into or out of a licensed occupation. Both approaches do more to account for differences between licensed and unlicensed workers that the first set of estimates cited above. These approaches typically find more modest impacts – under 10 percent – of licensing on wages, but some estimates show no significant impact at all.[27]

There has been less research on the impact that State licensing has on interstate mobility, but this too is a key outcome since mobility can contribute to wage growth for workers and economic recovery for local markets.[28] One study examines data on 14 occupations and finds that more restrictive State licensing statutes reduce interstate migration.[29] Forthcoming analysis of five licensed occupations finds that, controlling for observable differences that could affect migration rates, individuals in three of these occupations have lower *interstate* migration rates than their peers in other occupations, while their *intrastate* migration rates are similar.[30] This is to be expected if a State-based licensure system depressed mobility. Workers licensed in a given State face no added costs to intrastate moves, which do not affect their licensed status, but typically do bear substantial costs of re-licensing after an interstate move. Comparable unlicensed workers, by contrast, face no licensing-related costs to either type of move, and should consequently migrate across State lines at a higher rate than licensed workers.

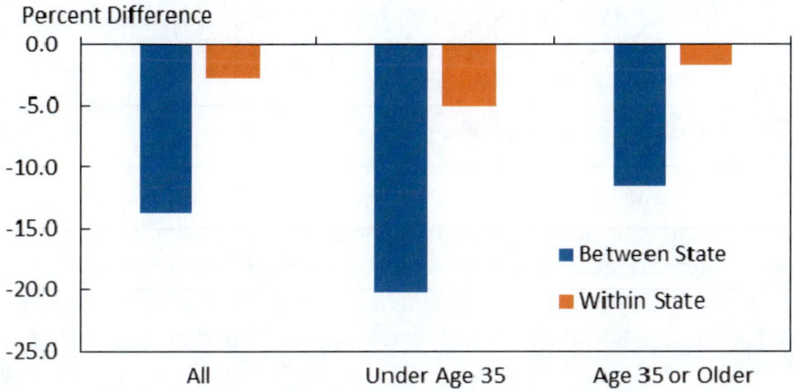


Sources: Census Bureau, American Community Survey 2010-2013; CEA Calculations. Number is calculated from an OLS regression controlling for race, citizenship, sex, citizenship, number of children, marital status, education, income, year, and state. Ages 25 to 65 were included.

Figure 1. Difference in Migration Rates of Workers on Most vs. Least Licensed Occupations.

To help fill this gap in the literature, we have carried out our own analysis. As shown in Figure 1 below, there are substantial differences in the likelihood of moving across State lines between workers in highly licensed occupations versus other workers, while there are only modest differences between the two groups in the likelihood of moving within a State. The figure shows that interstate migration rates for workers in the most-licensed occupations are lower by an amount equal to nearly 14 percent of the average migration rate compared to those in the least- licensed occupations. But the difference between these workers in within-State migration is much smaller, only about 3 percent of the average rate. These impacts are also much larger for younger licensed workers, in the age range where adult mobility is higher as workers are choosing where to start their careers. This difference is 20 percent of the average interstate migration rate for those under 35, compared to an impact of about 12 percent for workers over 35.

# II. THE PREVALENCE OF LICENSING: NATIONAL INCREASE, STATE DIFFERENCES

## The Increase in Licensing Over Time

Systematic data on who holds a license have been hard to come by until only very recently, making historical analysis difficult. What we know about the rise in licensing over time comes from the efforts of Kleiner and Krueger (2013), who chart the historical growth in licensing using a combination of data from the Council of State Governments, the Department of Labor, and two surveys that they commissioned through Gallup and Westat in 2006 and 2008, respectively. We reproduce their results below (Figure 2). Using their data, we show that the percentage of the workforce covered by State licensing laws grew from less than 5 percent in the early 1950s to 25 percent by 2008, meaning that the State licensing rate grew roughly five-fold during this period.[31]

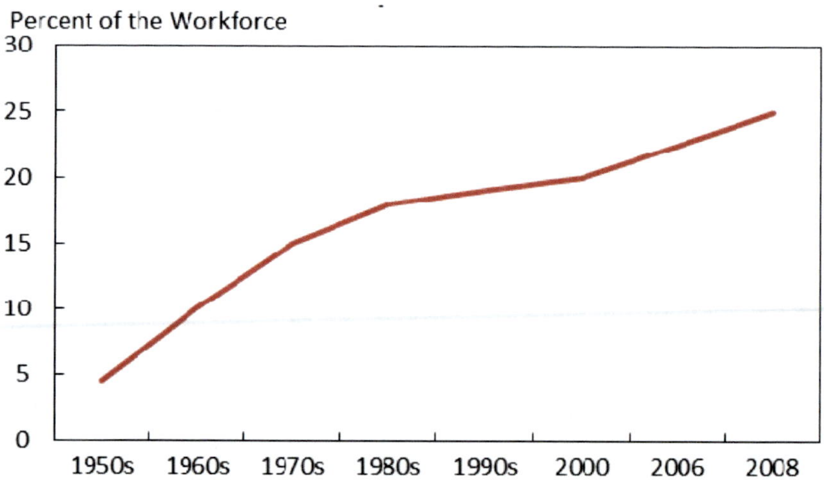


Sources: The Council of State Government (1952); Greene (1969); Kleiner (1990); Kleiner (2006); and Kleiner and Krueger (2013), Westat data; CEA Calculations.

Figure 2. Share of Workers with a State Occupational License.

The 2006 Gallup and 2008 Westat surveys were the first surveys to collect information on workers licensed at the local and Federal levels, in addition to those licensed by the States.[32] Although State licenses account for the bulk of licensing, the addition of local and Federal licensed occupations further raises the share of the workforce that is licensed to 29 percent.

More recent data on licensing prevalence come from a new module of the Census Bureau's Survey of Income and Program Participation (SIPP), the first large government survey to specifically ask questions about licensing and certification. In this source, 28 percent of civilian workers aged 18 through 64 had attained *a license or certification* in the fall of 2012, and about 20 percent were licensed.[33] However, because of the way the questions were posed, researchers analyzing this data cannot confidently distinguish between licensed and certified workers. Other limitations of the SIPP mean that it may be a less reliable source of information on licensing prevalence than Kleiner and Krueger's Westat survey, although gathering information on licensing in a major survey for the first time is certainly an important step in furthering research on these issues.[34]

## DATA ON WHO HOLDS A LICENSE

Two major sources of data on who holds a license are currently available for analysis: a dataset assembled for Kleiner and Krueger (2013) by Westat, and a survey module from the Survey of Income and Program Participation (SIPP). The Westat survey was designed by Kleiner and Krueger in order to precisely assess whether a survey respondent holds a license and to collect a modest set of labor market information from respondents. The SIPP is a U.S. Census Bureau survey that collects a large set of information on income, benefits use, living arrangements, and family structure but that has recently added questions relevant to worker licensing and certification. The SIPP questions, while useful, do not reliably distinguish licenses and certification. By contrast, the Westat survey asked whether a given credential was legally required for employment at the worker's current job, in order to distinguish between workers with licenses and those with certifications.

The two data sources have other strengths and weaknesses. The smaller Westat survey was short and focused – respondents were interviewed once and asked a total of 52 questions.

The SIPP is a more detailed longitudinal survey that follows the same households over multiple years. Though the SIPP's panel nature is an advantage in many contexts, it may be a liability in this case. The licensing and certification questions were asked after respondents had already answered the main SIPP questions, which generally take 30 to 40 minutes to answer.[a] The module was also added late in the SIPP panel, after attrition may have rendered the SIPP sample somewhat less representative of the overall population. On the other hand, the Westat survey was small, containing approximately 2,500 respondents, as compared to about 58,000 respondents in the SIPP module.

More government survey data will become available next year. The Current Population Survey began including three questions on certification and licensing in January 2015, and the data being collected will be made available for public use sometime in 2016.

[a] U.S. Census Bureau, private correspondence.

## Why Has Licensing Increased?

There are two ways to account for the increase in State licensing over the past few decades. One possibility is that this increase reflects changes in the composition of our workforce. Our economy has changed in significant ways since the 1950s, with employment shifting increasingly into services. As service sector workers are more likely to be licensed than workers in the goods- producing sector—32 percent of service sector workers are licensed compared to 16 percent of workers outside the service sector— this employment shift may therefore have increased the share of workers holding a license.[35] A second possibility is that more occupations have become licensed over time.

We first examine the role of the shift to services in raising licensing prevalence. For example, certain heavily-licensed professions in fields such as health and education have experienced substantial employment gains over the past few decades (Figure 3). The share of the workforce in the education and health fields rose from less than 13 percent in the late 1960s to over 22 percent today.

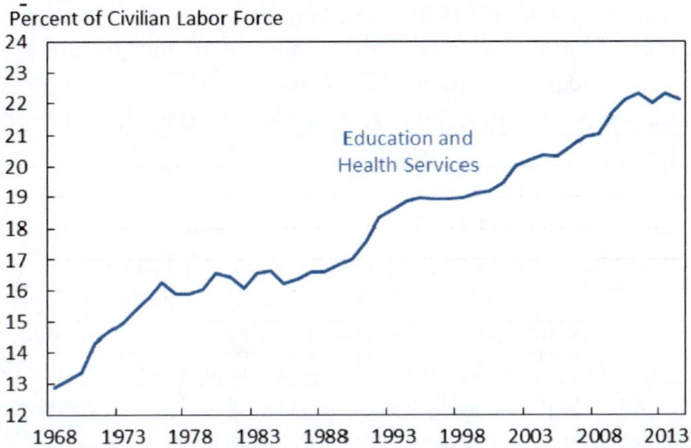


Source: Bureau of Labor Statistics; Current Population Survey, Annual Social and Economic Supplement; CEA calculations.

Figure 3. Share of Workforce in Education and Health Services.

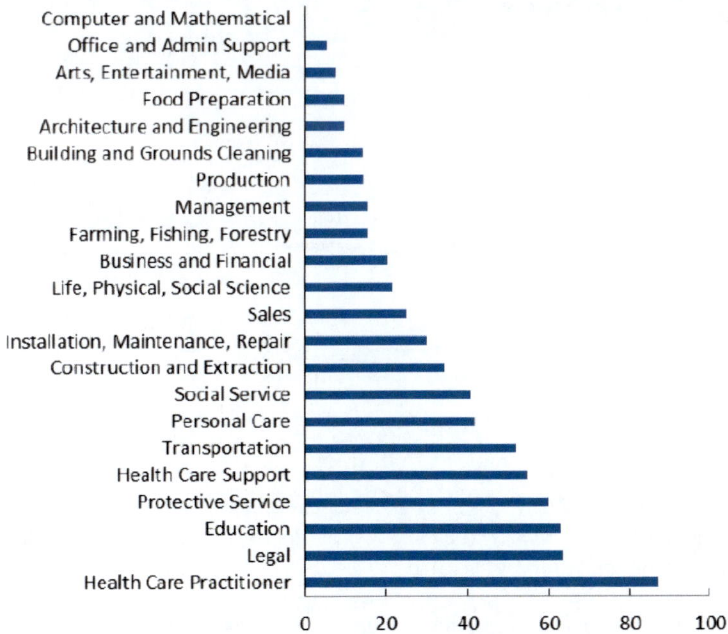


Source: Kleniner and Krueger (2013), Westat data; UST and CEA calculations.

Figure 4. Percent of Workers Licensed Within Occupation.

These fields, as shown below, have some of the highest rates of licensing in current data (Figure 4). More than 80 percent of health care practitioners report holding a license, and more than 60 percent of support workers in health care also hold licenses. Among workers in education, nearly 60 percent hold a license.

The growing share of workers in these heavily licensed occupations may therefore have contributed to the rise in licensing prevalence. However, analysis shows that this changing composition of the workforce can only explain part of the overall increase in licensing. Figure 5 compares the documented share of the licensed workforce to a series that adjusts for changes in workforce composition, but holds the fraction licensed in each occupation constant at 2008 levels.[36] The results suggest that only a little more than one-third of the increase in the percentage of workers licensed at the State level from the 1960s to the 2008 estimate is explained by the changing composition of the workforce. This means that the remaining two- thirds of the growth in licensing comes from an increase in the number of licensed professions.

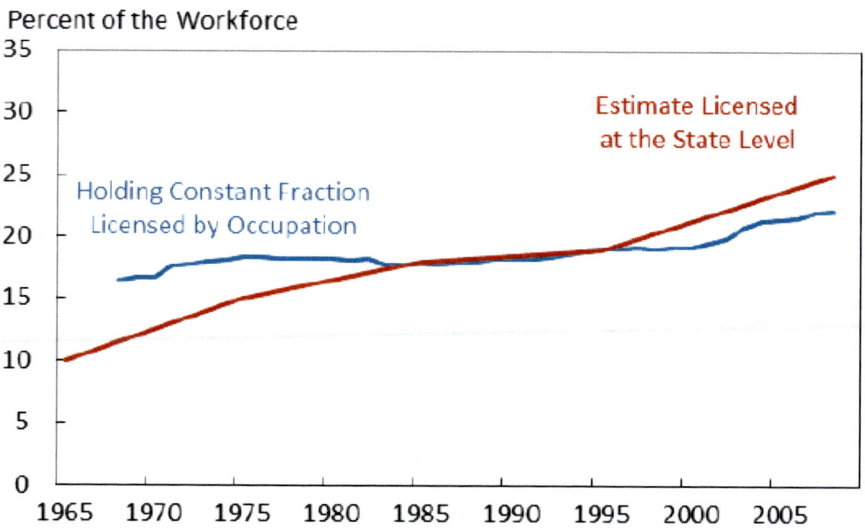


Source: Kleniner and Krueger (2013), Westat data; Bureau of Labour Statistices; Current Population Survey.

Figure 5. Percent Licensed Over Time: Estimated and Counterfactual.

Source: Kleiner and Krueger (2013) Westat data; Current Population Survey Outgoing Rotation Group; CEA calculations.

Figure 6. Share of All Licensed Workers in the 12 Occupations with the Most Licensed Workers.

The importance of an increase in the number of licensed occupations – not just the number of licensed workers – suggests that licensing has expanded considerably into sectors that were not historically associated with it. The figure below shows that among licensed workers today, fewer than half are in health care, education, and law— traditionally very highly licensed occupations. Instead, large shares of licensed workers today are in sales, management and even craft sectors like construction and repair.

A trend toward increasing skill and job training requirements over time may be one factor in the political process behind more licensing.[37] Conversations with regulators and industry groups indicate that practitioners in new fields often view licensing as one necessary step—along with others, such as forming professional schools, associations, and accreditation systems—toward achieving professionalization.[38] Following in the footsteps of more established professions such as physicians and lawyers, practitioners in newer areas may view professionalization as both beneficial for the profession—in helping to achieve greater legitimacy, cultural authority and income—as well as serving wider social interests, through improving quality and public safety.[39]

In addition, some argue that by identifying qualified practitioners, licensing can spur demand for licensed workers by reducing consumer uncertainty about the quality of the licensed service. In this way, licensing itself can increase the number of licensed workers.[40] Indeed, there is evidence from the turn of the 20th century that licensing was adopted in response to increased specialization and technological developments that made it more difficult for consumers to judge the quality of professional services.[41]

Others argue that producer groups tend to be much more politically influential than consumer groups. Licensing is a policy with concentrated benefits (for the licensed practitioners) and diffuse costs (for consumers and would-be practitioners). Thus, practitioners have a greater interest in licensing and may be better able to influence policy through their active professional associations.[42] Empirical work suggests that licensed professions' degree of political influence is one of the most important factors in determining whether States regulate an occupation.[43] These organizational factors may therefore also play a role in the overall rise in licensing.

Finally, licensing boards are often revenue neutral, and in some cases, even revenue- generating.[44] While there has been some movement over time away from funding licensing boards exclusively through fees, fees remain the primary funding mechanism.[45] Thus, legislators considering a new licensing proposal often do not have to grapple with the prospect of finding additional funding.

## Variation in Licensing across States

Recent evidence also shows that States vary dramatically in their rates of licensure, ranging from a low of 12 percent of workers in South Carolina to 33 percent in Iowa.[46] These large differences in licensing prevalence suggest that States are not treating occupations equivalently with regard to whether they do or do not require a license. For example, an Institute for Justice analysis of 102 low- and moderate-income occupations licensed in at least one State found that only 15 occupations were licensed in 40 States or more, and the average occupation was licensed in only 22 States.[47] In the figure below, we show the fraction of workers licensed in each State, using a new Harris survey used by Kleiner and Vorotnikov (2015). Many States have a licensed share that is 20 to

25 percent of their workforce, but three States license more than 30 percent of their workers and five States license less than 15 percent (Table 1).

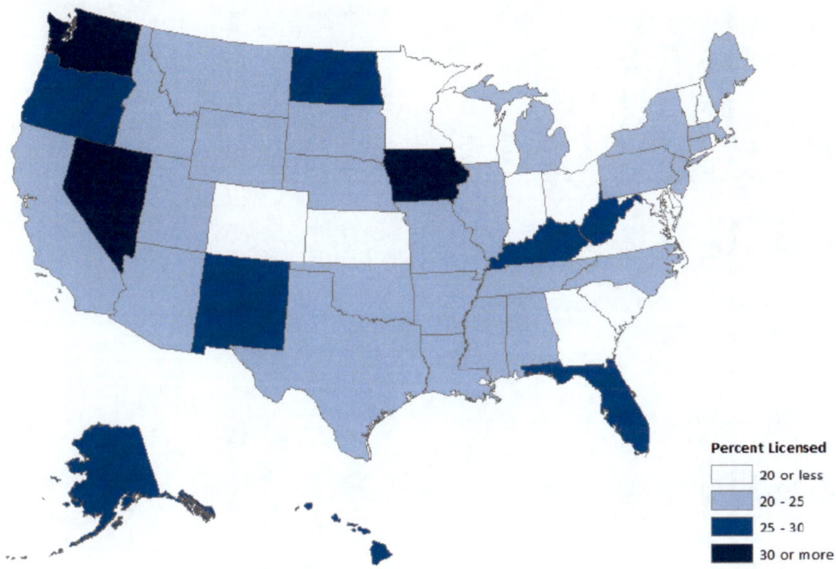


Source: Klenier and Vorotnikov (2015), Harris Data.

Figure 7. Percent of Workforce Licensed by State.

Interestingly, this variation in licensing prevalence appears not to be driven by differences in occupational mix across States. To see this, we used SIPP data to test how State licensing rates would change if every State had the same occupation mix but kept their own licensing rates within occupations. This resulting picture was very similar to the actual distribution of shares licensed across States in Figure 7, indicating that differences in occupational mix are not the primary determinant of State licensing differences.

### Table 1. Percent of Workforce Licensed by State

| State | Share Licensed | State | Share Licensed | State | Share Licensed | State | Share Licensed |
|---|---|---|---|---|---|---|---|
| Alabama | 20.9 | Illinois | 24.7 | Montana | 21.3 | Rhode Island | 14.5 |
| Alaska | 25.5 | Indiana | 14.9 | Nebraska | 24.6 | South Carolina | 12.4 |
| Arizona | 22.3 | Iowa | 33.3 | Nevada | 30.7 | South Dakota | 21.8 |
| Arkansas | 20.2 | Kansas | 14.9 | New Hampshire | 14.7 | Tennessee | 23.1 |
| California | 20.7 | Kentucky | 27.8 | New Jersey | 20.7 | Texas | 24.1 |
| Colorado | 17.2 | Louisiana | 22.3 | New Mexico | 25.9 | Utah | 23.8 |
| Connecticut | 24.7 | Maine | 20.7 | New York | 20.7 | Vermont | 16.8 |
| Delaware | 15.3 | Maryland | 17.2 | North Carolina | 22.0 | Virginia | 17.2 |
| District of Columbia | 19.7 | Massachusetts | 21.3 | North Dakota | 26.6 | Washington | 30.5 |
| Florida | 28.7 | Michigan | 20.6 | Ohio | 18.1 | West Virginia | 25.8 |
| Georgia | 15.7 | Minnesota | 15.0 | Oklahoma | 25.0 | Wisconsin | 18.4 |
| Hawaii | 26.6 | Mississippi | 23.1 | Oregon | 26.1 | Wyoming | 21.2 |
| Idaho | 22.8 | Missouri | 21.3 | Pennsylvania | 20.2 | | |

Source: Kleiner and Vorotnikov (2015), Harris data.

Note: Kleiner and Vorotnikov limited their analys is to individuals 18 or older who at the time of the survey were either currently employed or had been employed during the previous twelve months.

States vary not only in the share of workers with a license, but also in the difficulty of obtaining a license. State licensing laws vary in terms of the substantive requirements they impose, such as examinations, fees, minimum amounts of education, training or experience, language requirements, etc. The collection of these is sometimes called licensing burden. In practice, the extent to which licensing laws pose a barrier to entry depends on the stringency of these requirements. For example, while all States require manicurists to be licensed, some also require proof of English proficiency, and the required amount of training at a State-approved cosmetology school varies from 100 to 600 hours.

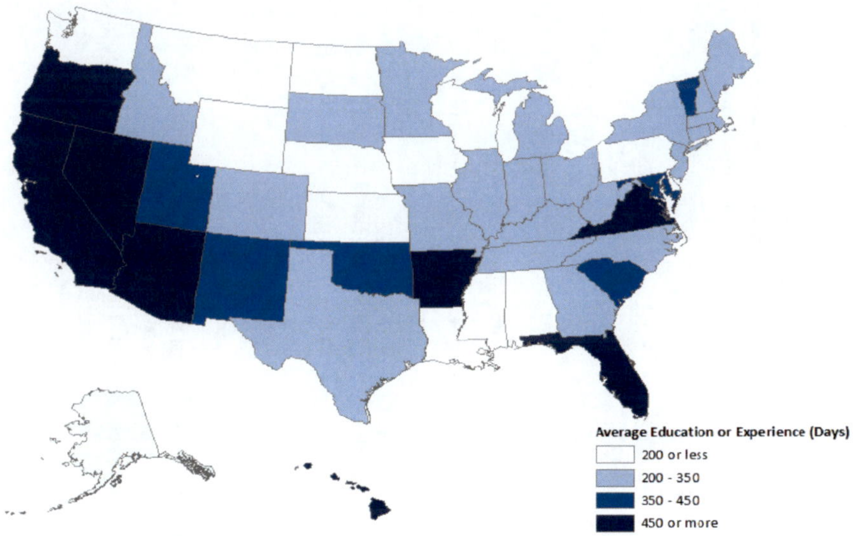


Source: Carpenter et al. (2012).

Note: Sample of 102 lower-and middle-skill occupations. Hours averaged over all licensed occupations from the sample of 102, by State.

Figure 8. Average Education or Experience Required for License by State for Selected Occupations.

Table 2. Education/Experience Burdens by State (Days)

| State | Days | State | Days | State | Days | State | Days |
|---|---|---|---|---|---|---|---|
| Alabama | 182.0 | Illinois | 203.0 | Montana | 133.0 | Rhode Island | 211.0 |
| Alaska | 179.0 | Indiana | 251.0 | Nebraska | 147.0 | South Carolina | 402.0 |
| Arizona | 599.0 | Iowa | 181.0 | Nevada | 601.0 | South Dakota | 271.0 |
| Arkansas | 689.0 | Kansas | 166.0 | New Hampshire | 230.0 | Tennessee | 222.0 |
| California | 549.0 | Kentucky | 324.0 | New Jersey | 292.0 | Texas | 326.0 |
| Colorado | 227.0 | Louisiana | 163.0 | New Mexico | 413.0 | Utah | 417.0 |
| Connecticut | 230.0 | Maine | 226.0 | New York | 283.0 | Vermont | 402.0 |
| Delaware | 195.0 | Maryland | 446.0 | North Carolina | 250.0 | Virginia | 462.0 |
| District of Columbia | 311.0 | Massachusetts | 293.0 | North Dakota | 132.0 | Washington | 199.0 |
| Florida | 603.0 | Michigan | 256.0 | Ohio | 341.0 | West Virginia | 247.0 |
| Georgia | 324.0 | Minnesota | 290.0 | Oklahoma | 416.0 | Wisconsin | 145.0 |
| Hawaii | 724.0 | Mississippi | 155.0 | Oregon | 568.0 | Wyoming | 196.0 |
| Idaho | 240.0 | Missouri | 220.0 | Pennsylvania | 113.0 | | |

Source: Carpenter et al., 2012.

Note: Sample of 102 lower- and middle-skill occupations. Hours averaged over all licensed occupations from the sample of 102, by state.

Though it is difficult to obtain comprehensive data on licensing burden, information collected by the Institute for Justice on 102 low- and medium-wage occupations provides a sense of the range of licensing burden across occupations and across States, in terms of education and experience prerequisites, licensure fees, examinations, and minimum age requirements. States range from Pennsylvania, where it takes an estimated average of 113 days (about four months) to fulfill the educational and experience requirements for the average licensed occupation examined, to Hawaii, where it takes 724 days (about two years).[48]

In addition to fulfilling these requirements, workers seeking a license face other procedural burdens, such as learning what the licensing requirements are and how to apply for a license, filling out the requisite paperwork, and waiting for their applications to be processed. These burdens are especially large for individuals with criminal records; it can take six months to a year for the relevant agency or board to review an applicant's criminal history and make an initial determination about whether she qualifies for a license.[49]

## III. Licensing and the Evolving Marketplace

While the basic economics behind licensing is the same now as five decades ago, the real world workplace has changed considerably. These changes have important implications for how to retain flexibility in the labor market while still using licensing to protect consumers. Some changes—like the rise of telework and distance learning—reflect new possibilities within the American economy. As the labor market changes, licensing rules set down in earlier decades may become an increasingly poor fit for the emerging occupational structure, necessitating continuing review and updates. On the other hand, other features of today's workplace reflect longer-run trends in which licensing may play a contributing role. For example, worker mobility in the United States has declined in the last several decades, and some have speculated as to whether the rise of licensing might be a driver of this trend.[50]

This section identifies several areas in which the U.S. workplace has undergone substantial change since licensing began to expand in the latter half of the 20th century. We discuss the key changes in each area and then explain how the current system of licensing poses challenges for each.

## The Rise of Telework

The same technology that allows workers in a large corporation to consult with clients and carry on other work remotely also allows the solo licensed practitioner to do similar tasks remotely. Falling costs of internet video-conferencing technology as well as simpler long-distance voice communication now allow licensed practitioners to consult easily across State lines.

Working from home is one indicator of the ability to do work from a distance, and this has been on the rise, with 44 percent more workers reporting that they work from home on a regular basis since 2001.[51] Moreover a large share of workers in highly licensed occupations say they have the ability to work from a remote location—particularly those in legal and social service occupations (see Figure 9 below).

Telework offers important opportunities for both licensed practitioners and their clients. Telework can enable more flexible scheduling and work locations, something that is important in helping workers with competing demands on their time stay in the labor force and maintain work-life balance. It has the potential to offer clients more continuous access to providers and access to more specialized providers, as well as increasing the pool of competing practitioners overall. Examples of the impact of telework on licensed occupations abound in the health care fields. Radiologists in Boston can now read x-rays and scans from locations as remote as Rwanda.[52] Insurance companies often provide clients access to a nurse-staffed call center to answer minor medical questions. These nurses reside and practice near the call center location, but they may take calls and make over-the-phone diagnoses for clients across the country. A study comparing telenursing from home versus from a call center found that nurses working from home were more productive and took fewer sick days, and they triaged patients with the same symptoms in a similar manner.[53]

However, while some States have made progress in adapting licensure requirements to allow for telework, practitioners are sometimes required to obtain licenses in every State where patients reside. In a 2009 report to Congress, the Department of Health and Human Services recommended expanding telehealth networks and reducing legal barriers, based on the effectiveness of telehealth in responding to public health emergencies and disasters. For example, events that require sheltering in place or quarantine may restrict access to health care. Telehealth applications including hotlines and interactive web-based programs were used extensively following the

September 11th, 2001 terrorist attacks on New York City and Washington, D.C., and during recent hurricanes. They have proven to be an effective means of providing large numbers of people spread out over great distances with information and guidance on how cope and care for themselves and others.[54]

The ability of licensed practitioners to provide services outside their jurisdictions of license raises questions about accountability for clients, since licensure is intended to protect the health and safety of the citizens of the State in which the license is held. The National Council of State Boards of Nursing was early to recognize this concern, and as part of their Nurse Licensure Compact, the participating States agreed that the State of practitioner residence should govern eligibility for a Compact (multi-state) license, though nurses working across state lines are also held accountable to the rules of the State in which they are practicing.[55]

State licensure has proven to be a barrier to the growth and development of telework in fields outside of health care as well. For example, clients can now use online document providers to produce certain kinds of legal documents, such as wills and trusts, or to file for a patent or trademark. However, such companies run the state-by-state risk of being found to have engaged in the unauthorized practice of law if they start offering a broader set of legal services.[56]

## The More Flexible Workplace and Scope of Practice

Licensing laws not only dictate whether an individual can practice at all, but also often determine what services she can provide as part of her practice. Regulations that place excessively stringent restrictions on practitioners' scope of practice can have effects very similar to the overall impact of licensing: limiting the supply of labor, restricting competition, increasing wages for incumbent practitioners but restricting access for others, and increasing the cost of services.[57] Scope of practice laws also vary from State to State, even though many professions have standardized nation-wide education standards and examinations.[58] The contents of these laws are a particular source of tension among groups of professions that provide complementary and sometimes overlapping or competing services, such as dentists and dental hygienists, doctors and advanced practice nurses, architects and interior designers, engineers and architects, and electricians and electrical engineers.[59]

Some scope of practice issues have arisen in response to concerns about the lack of affordable services, for example in law. Various State-level studies have found that a large proportion of the legal needs reported by low-income households goes unmet.[60] Data from court systems reveal large numbers of unrepresented or "pro se" litigants in courts. For example, a California study estimates that 67 percent of petitioners in family law cases were unrepresented, and over 90 percent of defendants in eviction cases were unrepresented.[61] A study in New York found that over 95 percent of people in eviction, child support, and consumer debt matters were unrepresented.[62] One survey found that 62 percent of judges said that pro se litigants were negatively impacted by their lack of representation.[63]

In an effort to help address these issues, the Supreme Court of Washington State in 2012 adopted a rule that created a new category of legal practitioners, "limited license legal technicians" (LLLTs) to provide certain limited kinds of legal services, such as preparing court documents and performing legal research, in approved areas. Other States may follow suit.[64] LLLTs are required to take about a year of classes at a community college, pass a licensing exam, and fulfill supervised experience requirements. The first area to be approved is family law.[65]

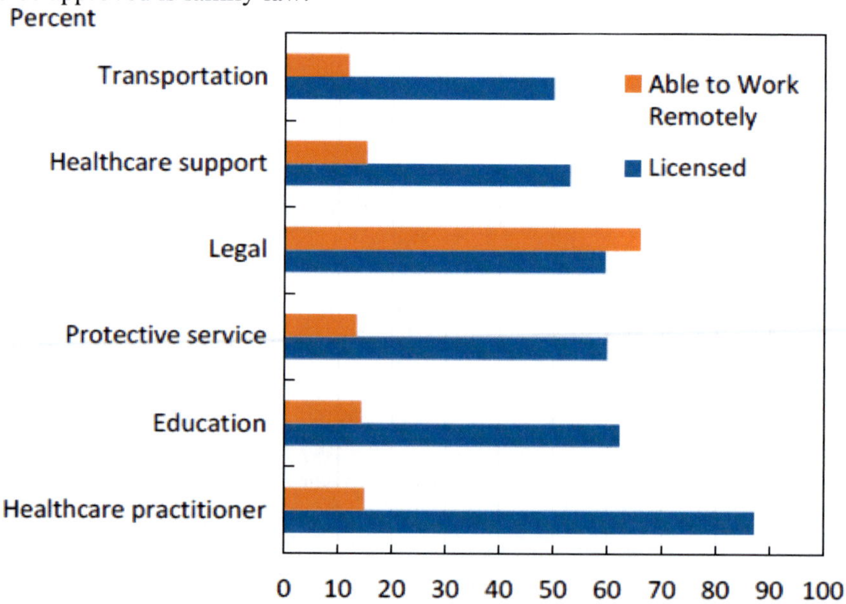


Source: Kleiner and Krueger (2013) Westat data; CEA calculations.

Figure 9. Licensing and Remote Work by Occupation.

Scope of practice has long been a particular focus in the health care context, in large part because of concerns about access to primary care. Current scope of practice laws for advanced practice registered nurses—nurses such as nurse practitioners (NPs) with master's degrees or more— vary dramatically by State, both in terms of their substantive content and the level of specificity that they provide.[66] But State-level evidence suggests that easing scope of practice laws for APRNs represents a viable means of increasing access to certain primary care services. Research finds that APRNs can provide a range of primary care services to patients as effectively as physicians.[67] Between 1998 and 2010, States with the least restrictive regulations of NPs (e.g., those not requiring physician supervision for practice or prescriptions) gained more licensed NPs per 100,000 residents, and patients in those States had a 2.5-fold greater likelihood of patients' receiving their primary care from NPs than did patients in the most restrictive States.[68] Stange (2014) finds that greater supply of NPs and physician assistants (PAs) has had minimal impacts on access to health care and utilization, but that expansions in prescriptive authority for NPs have been associated with modest increases in utilization.[69]

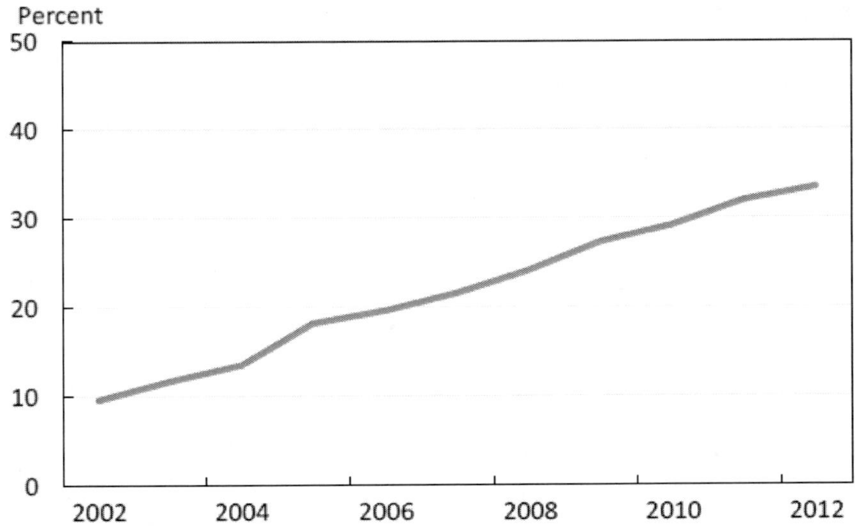


Source: Allen and Seaman (2014)

Figure 10. Online Learning Enrollment as a Share of Total Enrollment.

## The Arrival of Distance Learning

In 2013, 11.3 percent of all U.S. undergraduate students (2.0 million students) were enrolled in institutions in which all instructional content was delivered through distance education, and more than one in four undergraduates took at least one distance education course (4.6 million students).[70] Students can now take courses remotely from training providers in almost any State. The prevalence of online undergraduate education has grown dramatically since 2002 (see Figure 10).[71]

Online courses offer many opportunities for students to gain skills at low cost while following a flexible schedule. They can also help State higher education systems reduce duplication of narrow training programs through the use of reciprocal recognition of online coursework obtained through another State's system. And the rate of online course usage is high among students in the heavily licensed fields of health (33 percent) and law (43 percent), although clinical components of training in these fields cannot be completed online.[72]

Distance education is also a commonly used practice for continuing professional education in licensed occupations. All States and some U.S. territories currently mandate some form of continuing medical education for re-licensure; continuing education is also common in nursing, accounting, and in the legal profession.[73] Many providers are online or distance providers, which may be the most convenient option for professionals for whom taking time away from the office to attend classes or in-person trainings can be costly.

Occupational licensing boards' practices may affect students' participation in distance education. Many nurse licensing boards automatically accept degrees and credentials from a list of preapproved schools, which tend to be schools with physical locations in-state.[74] Although some accept degrees from out-of-state institutions, these degrees may need to go through additional accreditation, for example by an outside group like the Accreditation Commission for Education in Nursing. If the State of the licensing board and the State of the educational institution are both part of the National Council for State Authorization Reciprocity Agreements (NC-SARA) (see box below), however, accreditation by the State of the educational institution serves as accreditation in the State of the licensing board. However, in some States where these forms of accreditation of an out-of-state institutions is not possible, a nursing student may have to get a license in the State of their institution and have it transferred through an endorsement process to the State where they want to practice. In some cases, these requirements may create additional hurdles for students who take advantage of distance education.

### The National Council for State Authorization Reciprocity Agreements

The National Council for State Authorization Reciprocity Agreements (NC-SARA) provides a standardized means of accrediting distance education programs across all member States (of which there are 23), making it easier for distance education institutions to gain accreditation in multiple States – in the past, institutions had to go through the application process of each of the States and territories separately.[a]

Under NC-SARA standardization, accredited institutions can more easily offer distance education programs in more States, thus giving each State that is a member of NC-SARA access to more distance education programs, increasing the size of the market and providing students with more choices. States that join NC- SARA must agree to a number of requirements. Most importantly, they must demonstrate an acceptable process for approving in-State institutions for SARA participation, and they must task a State agency with housing and administering SARA activities, including resolution of student complaints.

[a] See nc-sara.org for more information. National Council for State Authorization Reciprocity Agreements. http://nc- sara.org/.

## The Emergence of Consumer Information and Review Markets

Consumers often rely on reputations when first choosing a service provider, be that a doctor, a hair stylist, or a home contractor. Yet consumers do not always have enough information to accurately judge providers' quality. In these cases, occupational licensing or certification can potentially provide a means of ensuring quality or helping consumers to identify high-quality providers. In recent years, however, the growth of online consumer information and review websites has made it easier for consumers to find information on the quality of firms and practitioners, and some observers have argued that consumer protection regulation should be updated to reflect this new access to information.[75]

On the other hand, online reputational sites also have limitations in their ability to inform consumers. Participants may have an incentive to game their ratings, reducing the confidence consumers place in them.[76] Quality may not always be apparent even after the service has been received, and the way that information is presented can have a substantial impact on how consumers interpret and respond to it.[77] Thus, there continues to be an important role for appropriately targeted regulation in protecting consumers.

## Licensing for Workers with a Criminal Record

In many cases, a criminal record is an obstacle to obtaining a license. Data from the American Bar Association show that individuals with felonies are ineligible for thousands of professional licenses and certifications.[78] For example, individuals with a felony are ineligible for a land surveyor license in Alabama or an optometry license in California.[79]

These exclusions have far-reaching implications. It is estimated that between 70 and 100 million Americans (as many as one in three) have a criminal record.[80] Around 688,000 individuals were released from Federal and State prisons in 2011, nearly all of whom will need to seek employment.[81] Laws restricting licensing opportunities for workers with criminal records have a disproportionate impact on Black and Hispanic workers.[82] Many of these individuals have criminal histories which should not automatically disqualify them from work in a licensed profession.

While it is understandable that some kinds of criminal convictions should disqualify applicants for certain kinds of jobs, in many cases, a criminal conviction *of any kind* may be a bar to licensure. Twenty-five States and the District of Columbia have no standards in place governing the relevance of conviction records of applicants for occupational licenses. In these States, a licensing board may deny a license to an applicant who has a criminal conviction, regardless of whether the conviction is relevant to the license sought, how recent it was, or whether there were any extenuating circumstances. In many States, employers and occupational licensing boards are also permitted to ask about and consider arrests that never led to a conviction in making their employment decision.[83]

In contrast, 25 States have standards in place that require some kind of relationship between the license sought and the applicant's criminal history. For instance, the Texas Occupations Code states that "each licensing authority shall issue guidelines… [stating] the reasons a particular crime is considered to relate to a particular license."[84] While some offenses, like homicide and assault, are disqualifying crimes for many licenses in Texas, other offenses only disqualify applicants for specific licenses for which the conviction is relevant. For example, the Texas Occupations Code provides that a conviction for animal cruelty is a basis for denying or revoking a licensed breeder license, while a conviction for driving while intoxicated is a basis for denying a tow truck operators' license.[85]

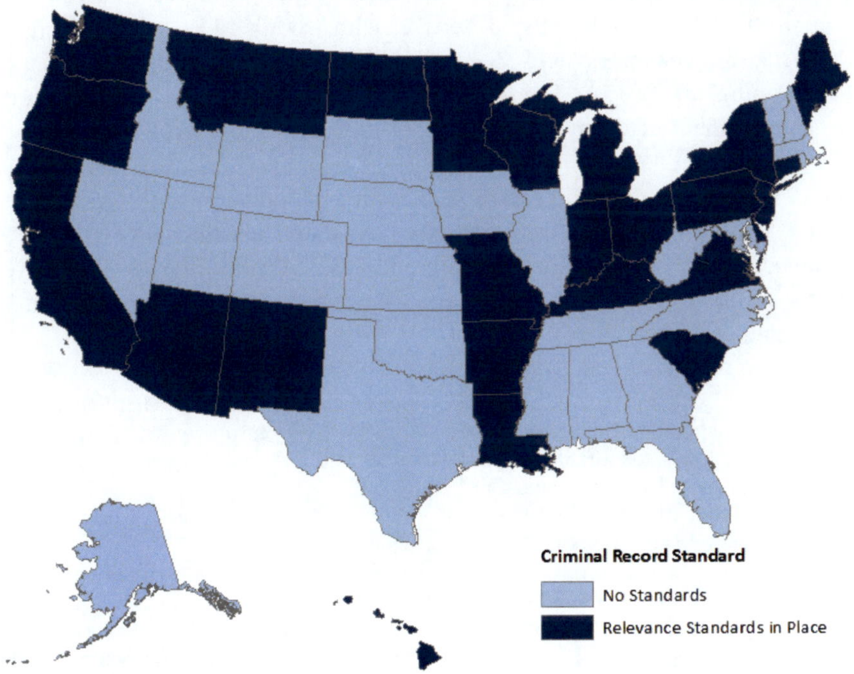


Source: Legal Action Center.

Figure 11. Standards Governing Relevance of Conviction Records of Applicants for Occupational licensure.

## REVOCATION OF LICENSES FOR STUDENT LOAN DEFAULT

In 21 States, defaulting on student loan debt can result in the suspension or revocation of a worker's occupational license.[a] This policy affects a large segment of the population, as the student loan market has experienced substantial growth in recent years. Between 2000 and 2015, the size of the student loan market increased by 170 percent in inflation-adjusted terms, with roughly $1.1 trillion in outstanding balances held by over 41 million individuals as of the beginning of 2015.[b] The policy is also misguided, as losing an occupational license may make it more difficult for the worker to repay a student loan.

However, interest in reform is building. Montana recently passed a law ending this practice, with one legislator arguing that it was unnecessarily punitive and counterproductive.[c] A bill to repeal a similar law in Iowa was recently drafted, but did not make it out of the legislature.[d]

[a] National Consumer Law Center. 2014. State Laws and Statutes That Suspend Professional Licenses and Certificates. http://www.jwj.org/wp-content/uploads/2015/02/State-Laws-and-Statutes-That-Suspend-Professional-Licenses-and-Certificates.pdf.

[b] Department of Education 4 percent sample of National Student Loan Data System data; Office of Tax Analysis calculations.

[c] Montana Legislature. 2015. House Bill 363. http://leg.mt.gov/bills/2015/billhtml/HB0363.htm; Whitney, Eric. 2015. "States Review Laws Revoking Licenses for Student Loan Defaults." NPR. http://www.npr.org/2015/04/08/398037156/States-review-laws-revoking-licenses-for-student-loan-defaults.

[d] Iowa Legislature. 2015. House File 196. http://coolice. legis. iowa. gov/CoolICE/default.asp?Category=billinfo&Service=Billbook&menu=false&hbill=HF196.

## Licensing for Foreign Immigrants

Many immigrants arrive in the United States having already completed extensive education, job training, or work experience abroad. For example, 30 percent of working-age immigrants in 2010 had at least a college degree. However, research indicates that high-skilled immigrants have a hard time finding employment that allows them to make full use of their skills. Hall et al. (2011) find that nearly half of immigrants with a bachelor's degree are overqualified for their current jobs, compared to around one-third of their native-born counterparts, resulting in underutilization of valuable skills.[86]

One likely contributing factor is that immigrants must often complete duplicative and costly requirements in order to acquire a U.S. license in their chosen career. In many cases, the training or experience that these immigrants acquired overseas does not count toward fulfilling the relevant licensing requirements. For example, in Illinois, if an engineer earns a degree from most universities abroad, she must submit proof that she worked under a U.S. engineer for four years; other work experience abroad will not suffice.[87]

Licensing requirements that prevent qualified immigrants from finding employment in their chosen profession affect not only the immigrant workers themselves, but also consumers. Removing such requirements has the potential to improve access to services, especially among those at the middle and lower-end of the income distribution.[88]

## Declining Mobility in the U.S. Labor Force

Licensed workers are less likely to move over longer distances, notably across State lines. As discussed earlier, it can be difficult to know what to make of this comparison, since individuals willingly choose lines of work with the understanding that these do or do not require State licensing. However, as discussed above, the similar rates at which unlicensed and licensed workers move within States suggests that those workers may not actually be very different in their desire to move. Rather, the large difference in *interstate* migration rates further suggests that licensing constitutes a significant barrier to relocation.

Many workers may choose their occupation with the understanding that it requires a State license, but life events can intervene to change their expectations about the need to make a cross-state move. For example, military spouses may have entered their field before marriage. Other events – like a local disaster or a health crisis for a parent – may mean that workers who had never planned to move across State lines after receiving a license suddenly find themselves needing to do so. In such cases, the need to re-license is an important concern. If States don't offer a temporary license to practice (while re-certifying), then the financial barriers of licensing are even more significant.

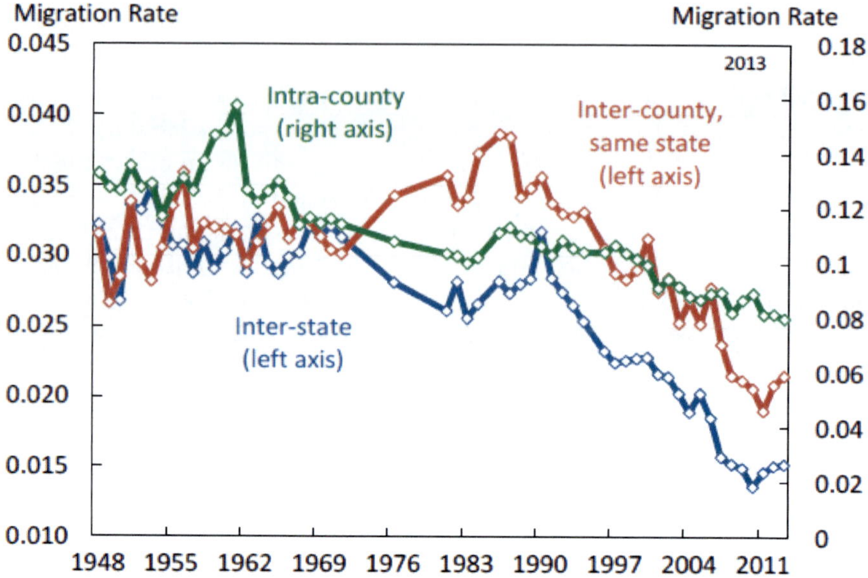


Source: Molloy, Smith, and Wozniak (2014).

Note. Migration rates of the civilian population age 16 and up from the Current Population Survey. Post-1989 migration rates are calculated from microdata and exclude imputed values. Sample details are given in Molloy, Smith and Wozniak (2011) and Saks and Wozniak (2011).[91]

Figure 12. Migration Rates by Distance.

There are clear benefits to mobility, both for workers, employers, and the economy at large, and limits to mobility are themselves a cause for concern. At the very least, the restrictions on mobility should be weighed as costs, both to a State's own population and to employers in that State who may be seeking to hire licensed workers from a broader, national labor pool. However, overall geographic mobility has been declining since the 1970s in the United States, as shown below.[89] It is unlikely that licensing is the sole driver of this change – the rise in licensing pre- dates the decline by at least two decades and short-distance moves have declined alongside long-distance moves – but licensing may play a contributing role, as posited by Davis and Haltiwanger (2014).[90]

## INTERSTATE MEDICAL LICENSURE COMPACT (IMLC)

As of May 2015, an interstate compact has gone into effect for physicians in nine States, with more States expected to join over the next year. It is organized somewhat differently from the Nurse Licensure Compact (NLC). Rather than creating a separate interstate license that can be used in multiple States, as the NLC does, the IMLC will make it easier for physicians to acquire many individual State licenses at once.[a] They will have full rights to practice in States for which they obtain a license, regardless of permanent residence. Fees will still be payable to each jurisdiction in which a license is acquired.

However, like the updated NLC, the Interstate Medical Licensure Compact will be a two-tiered system. Only physicians who meet relatively stringent requirements will be permitted to participate in the compact, but other doctors will still be able to acquire State licenses under the pre-existing regime.

[a] Chaudhry, Humayun J., Lisa A. Robin, Eric M. Fish, Donald H. Polk, and J. Daniel Gifford. 2015. "Improving Access and Mobility – The Interstate Medical Licensure Compact." *The New England Journal of Medicine* 372, no. 17: 1581-1583.

# IV. LICENSING REFORMS

The prior sections have described the growth in licensing and the impacts that licensing may have on employment, worker mobility, and the price of goods and services, as well as special burdens that licensing may place on specific populations, such as those with criminal records, military spouses, teleworkers, entrepreneurs, and low-wage workers. These concerns need to be weighed against the goals of promoting consumer health and safety as well as other professional objectives that groups may seek with licensing. Recognizing that, in many cases, the costs and benefits of licensing are not appropriately weighed, State policymakers and industry representatives are spearheading a number of reform efforts to promote a more thoughtful approach to licensing.

Although licensing policy falls in the purview of individual States, the Federal government can help to facilitate State reforms by providing information and resources to States. The President's FY2016 Budget includes

$15 million in new discretionary funding at the Department of Labor to identify, explore, and address areas where licensing requirements create barriers to labor market entry or labor mobility. This builds on the progress that the Office of the First Lady and Dr. Biden have made through the Joining Forces initiative to work with States to reduce licensing barriers for veterans and military spouses.

This section enumerates a number of considerations that policymakers should take into consideration in order to ensure that occupational regulation serves the public interest. It also outlines some promising efforts to improve our system of licensing, and describes several Federal initiatives to promote licensing reform. Based on existing research and conversations with policymakers and industry representatives from over 25 States, we present a number of practices that may lead to more transparent and effective licensing systems. We then discuss several of these proposals in more detail.

## Framework for Licensing Reform

Because occupations are diverse in their tasks, aims and responsibilities, successfully regulating them often requires a tailored approach. Nevertheless, there are a number of common factors that policymakers contemplating enacting, revising, or repealing an occupational regulation must consider. We summarize these factors in the box below and discuss them in more detail in the text that follows.

## Discussion of Selected Best Practices and Examples

As discussed above, applying certain best practices in occupational licensing can ensure that public safety and health needs are met while maintaining flexibility in the labor market and opportunities for workers. Below we provide more detail on how State governments could apply these practices to their occupational licensing systems, as well as examples of current State initiatives to build a more modern regulatory structure.

## LICENSING BEST PRACTICES

### Ensure that Licensing Restrictions are Closely Targeted to Protecting Public Health and Safety, and are Not Overly Broad or Burdensome

1. In cases where public health and safety concerns are mild, consider using alternative systems that are less restrictive than licensing, such as voluntary State certification ("right-to-title") or registration (filing basic information with a State registry).
2. Make sure that substantive requirements of licensing (e.g., education and experience requirements) are closely tied to public health and safety concerns.
3. Minimize procedural burdens of acquiring a license, in terms of fees, complexity of requirements, processing time, and paperwork.
4. Where licensure is deemed appropriate, allow all licensed professionals to provide services to the full extent of their current competency, even if this means that multiple professions provide overlapping services.
5. Review licensing requirements for the formerly incarcerated, immigrants, and veterans to ensure that licensing laws do not prevent qualified individuals from securing employment opportunities, while still providing appropriate protections for consumers.

### Facilitate a Careful Consideration of Licensure's Costs and Benefits

1. Carry out comprehensive cost-benefit assessments of licensing laws through both sunrise and regular sunset reviews, incorporating criteria like:
   - The presence of legitimate public health and safety concerns or substantial fiduciary responsibilities;
   - Whether existing legal remedies, consumer rating and reputational mechanisms, and less-burdensome regulatory approaches are adequate to protect consumers;

- Whether the proposed licensing requirements are actually well-tailored to ensure quality and protect consumers;
- The effect that the license would have on practitioner supply;
- The effect that the license would have on the price of goods and services; and
- Administrative costs of enforcing the license.

2. Evidence suggests that removing licenses is much more difficult than enacting them, so sunset reviews in particular may be ineffective without certain protections. To strengthen both sunset and sunrise reviews, consider taking such measures as:
   - Providing agencies or sunrise and sunset commissions responsible for conducting the cost-benefit analysis with adequate resources;
   - Ensuring that the cost-benefit review process is insulated against political interference;
   - Legislating that a minimum number of votes be required to overrule the sunrise or sunset agency's recommendation;
   - Appointing specialized committees within State legislatures that are responsible for all licensing issues, and that will work with the State agency in charge of conducting the review.
3. Promote the appointment of public representatives to licensing boards, alongside professional members.

## Work to Reduce Licensing's Barriers to Mobility

1. Harmonize licensing requirements to the maximum extent possible across States.
2. Form interstate compacts that make it easier for licensed workers to practice and relocate across State lines, while also enabling State regulators to share practitioners' performance histories.
3. When forming such an interstate arrangement, avoid categorically excluding individuals with a criminal record or adopting the licensing requirements of the most stringent participating States.

4. If agreeing on common standards for interstate licenses is difficult, consider a "two-tiered" structure that allows States with more flexible requirements to retain their rules while restricting interstate reciprocity to workers who satisfy a higher bar.

***Ensure that Licensing Restrictions are Closely Targeted to Protecting Public Health and Safety, and are Not Overly Broad or Burdensome***

**Consider Alternative Forms of Occupational Regulations**

Other regulatory options short of licensing are generally available.[92] These options include certification (whether private or government-administered), registration, bonding and insurance, and inspection, among others. These alternatives may vary in terms of the burdens they place on workers, and may be more effective in targeting different types of regulatory problems. For instance, regular inspection of business establishments can be an effective means of enforcing health and safety restrictions.

- *Certification,* or "right-to-title," restricts the use of a profession's title to those who have been certified, but allows anyone to perform the duties of the profession, regardless of whether they have been certified or not. By restricting use of a title to workers who have achieved certain minimum requirements, certification may represent a less restrictive means of providing consumers with information regarding provider quality. Regulation through certification provides information to consumers while allowing them to choose the quality they can afford, and does so without limiting workers' access to the occupation. Thus, for occupations where the consequences of low quality service are not severe, voluntary certification from a private or public accreditor may in some cases be more appropriate than licensing. Certification is less appropriate, however, when the public is likely to make improper or dangerous decisions, and when these decisions might have spillover consequences for others.[93] Certification should reflect overall practitioner quality, and States should consider including a mechanism for evaluating and revoking certification when a practitioner no longer meets the quality standards.
- *Registration* – simply maintaining a list of practitioners – is useful for ensuring that providers are easily reached in the case of a complaint. It can also provide needed information about labor supply in an

occupation to State data agencies. Registration can be combined with some minimum standards, such as providing documentation for qualification or a character reference, that are typically less burdensome than those required by licensing.

- *Mandatory bonding*, with or without insurance, is another alternative. With bonding, employers or workers are required to maintain funds against which consumer claims can be made. This both communicates confidence in the expected quality of work and ensures that consumers will be compensated in the event they suffer harm. Alternatively, a worker or firm may purchase insurance. This serves a similar purpose, with the insurance company's willingness to sell a policy itself signaling confidence in the expected quality of work.
- *Direct regulation of firms and establishments*, in particular through inspection, in many instances may be more effective and less burdensome than licensing. As discussed above, licensing requirements are not always tied to quality improvements, and licensing boards are often not diligent in monitoring and disciplining licensed practitioners.[94] By contrast, direct regulation of establishments can result in more regular monitoring and inspection without excluding practitioners from the labor force. For example, establishments that serve alcoholic beverages are often regulated at the establishment level, while service workers are often unlicensed.

In weighing the most appropriate form of regulation, policymakers should also account for the costs of administering and enforcing the regulation. These costs vary depending on the content of licensing requirements and activities of the boards. For instance, licensing boards will often oversee entrance requirements regarding education and experience, set rules for other States' licensees, and hear complaints against violators of licensing regulations.

Some States have implemented or are considering adopting alternative regulatory approaches. For example, in 2015, the Indiana legislature passed a law that sets up a pilot program that would create a State registry of privately certified individuals. Occupations that are currently licensed will be unaffected (as will workers in health care occupations), but associations that privately certify workers in currently unlicensed fields will be able to apply to have their certification count as "State registered." Conditional on meeting a set of requirements, certified workers will then have exclusive right to use the title "State registered," but not an exclusive right to practice.[95]

In conversations with State regulators, they have suggested that some professionals have been seeking licensing not because unlicensed practitioners are a threat to public safety, but because third-parties won't recognize unlicensed practitioners in situations such as reimbursement for services. In these cases, States may want to engage with third-party payers to identify and address appropriate paths forward.

## Reducing the Substantive and Procedural Burdens of Professional Regulations

Regardless of whether a profession is licensed or certified, it is important that the application process be as straightforward and transparent as possible, and that the requirements for obtaining a license or certification be narrowly tied to the specific public health and safety concerns of the work. There are two ways in which requirements tend to drift from these objectives. The first is when practitioners, often through the regulatory boards they participate in, act to raise standards. For example, the American Physical Therapy Association has considered requiring a bachelor's degree for obtaining a physical therapist assistant license.[96] Regulatory agencies also sometimes apply the requirements of an older occupation to a new but related type of work. For example, the "corporate practice of law" doctrine, which prohibits non-lawyers from participating in the financing, ownership, or management of law businesses, has been applied to online legal document and information companies seeking to provide online legal assistance or other innovative products.[97] These services are related to the activities of lawyers but are legitimately new forms of work that merit separate consideration of the need for licensing.

Also, the labor market effects of specific occupational regulations sometimes depend less on their formal category than on other factors, such as their substantive and procedural requirements, as well as norms within the labor market. For example, a doctor who is not "board- certified" may find it difficult to obtain or maintain a position for practice in a hospital.[98] By contrast, if a particular license is not well-enforced, or if it imposes only minimal substantive requirements (e.g., educational and training standards) and is procedurally very easy to obtain (for example, it entails minimal paperwork and processing time), then it may have less of an impact on workers and consumers.

## STREAMLINING REQUIRED TRAINING TO FOCUS ON HEALTH AND SAFETY

The Professional Beauty Association (PBA) represents a variety of professions related to personal appearance: cosmetologists, barbers, hairdressers, and manicurists, among others. Cosmetologists are uniformly licensed, though requirements vary substantially across States, with some requiring more than twice as much education as others. On average, more than a year of education is required, with fees that are often non-trivial.

The PBA is now pushing for two general types of reform in the licensing of cosmetologists. First, they are seeking to standardize requirements for hours of schooling across States. This should eventually help make it simpler for workers to move across States. Second, they are advocating for licensing qualifications (mostly related to required school curriculum) that are more closely aligned with public health and safety concerns. This second initiative in particular is an important step forward for licensing reform.

Many occupations have educational requirements that are not necessary to promote public safety. Limiting licensing requirements to those that are necessary to protect the public can go a long way towards achieving a rational, minimally-intrusive licensing regime.

**Allow Licensed Professionals to Provide Services to the Full Extent of their Current Competency**

When licensing is deemed appropriate for a given occupation, policymakers must also determine the boundaries of the licensed activity, or "scope of practice." Typically, this becomes an important issue when multiple licensed occupations provide complementary or overlapping services. For instance, physicians and nurse practitioners may both prescribe medicines in some States. According to the Pew Health Professions Committee report in 1995, policymakers should endeavor to allow practitioners to offer services to the full extent of their competency and knowledge, even if this means that multiple professions are licensed to offer overlapping services.[99]

While most States simply focus on scope of practice on a case-by-case basis, a few States have recently considered their scope of practice rules in a more comprehensive manner, primarily in the health care context. In 2007, Pennsylvania expanded the types of services that can be provided by physician assistants, advanced practice nurses, physical therapists, and pharmacists. In

2008, the Colorado Governor commissioned a committee to investigate options for improving utilization of non-physician providers. In New Mexico, an interim legislative committee was established to help legislators evaluate proposed scope of practice reforms. Minnesota and California both have agencies that review scope of practice rules and potential policy changes.[100]

Connecticut's State legislature conducted a particularly thorough 2009 review of scope of practice for the health care professions, including comparisons with regulatory models from other States.[101] In keeping with the academic literature, Connecticut's report emphasizes the importance of evaluating scope of practice implications for consumer access to care. It also recommends that the legislature set up a process by which any health care profession could submit a request to change its scope of practice. Since 2012, the scope of practice review committee has received 21 requests from different health care occupations' associations through this process and has ruled on 6 of them.[102]

## Easing Exclusions for Workers with Criminal Records

Occupational licenses are often unavailable to workers with criminal records.[103] Licensing regulations often refer broadly to "good moral character" as a requirement for holding a license, and in practice this has in many cases been interpreted to ban individuals with any criminal record.[104] Policymakers should endeavor to strike a more appropriate balance between protecting the public and ensuring that licensing laws do not prevent qualified individuals from securing employment opportunities. First, policymakers should refrain from categorically excluding individuals with criminal records, and instead should only exclude those individuals whose convictions are recent and relevant, and pose a legitimate threat to public safety. Second, it is important that workers are provided with a timely right to appeal and seek waivers from criminal background exclusions. Finally, it is important that licensing boards provide transparent and clear explanations of their background check requirements.[105]

### *Facilitate a Careful Consideration of Licensure's Costs and Benefits*

## Sunset and Sunrise Reviews

Many States conduct "sunrise" or "sunset" reviews of occupational licensure. Both sunrise and sunset reviews subject licensing frameworks to a cost-benefit analysis. Sunrise reviews trigger cost-benefit analysis when a new licensing proposal is enacted, while sunset reviews apply cost- benefit analysis to licensing laws that have been in place for some time. Currently, 13 States have in place some sort of sunrise law, while 32 States maintain some sort of sunset process and 10 States have both.[106]

States vary in how thoroughly and independently they administer sunrise and sunset reviews. Ideally, during a sunrise or sunset review, analysts would estimate the costs and benefits of the licensing proposal or legislation in a careful and thorough manner, comparing licensing with alternative regulatory options, as well as legislative inaction. Florida, for instance, requires in its Sunrise Act that licensure only be used when "the overall cost-effectiveness and economic impact of the proposed regulation, including the indirect costs to consumers, will be favorable" and "other types of less restrictive regulation would not effectively protect the public."[107] Longer- term reviews of licensing are especially useful, since the labor market and quality impacts of licensing may only materialize gradually over time.

There is some evidence to suggest that sunrise reviews can be more successful at limiting the growth of licensing than sunset reviews are at removing unnecessary licensing. Thornton and Timmons (2015) discover only eight instances in the past 40 years of the successful "de-licensing" of an occupation at the State level, and in four of these cases, attempts to relicense the occupations followed afterward. They find that State sunset committees usually recommend the continuation of the license, and that in the rare instances when they recommend that licensing laws be repealed, the State legislature usually ignores the recommendation.[108] Conversations with State regulators also suggested that sunrise review may be more efficacious than sunset review.

Since 1995, Maine's Department of Professional and Financial Regulation has conducted a sunrise review of any proposed legislation that would establish an occupational licensing board or expand a current practitioner's scope of practice. Depending on the type of profession to be regulated, the sunrise process can take up to a year for research to be conducted and for a legislative committee to evaluate the proposal based on 13 review criteria and make a final decision whether to regulate the profession. According to Maine's Department of Professional and Financial Regulation, only one occupation has acquired a licensed status in the past 15 years.[109]

A sunset review can nevertheless be useful because, even if licensing was justified when first introduced, technological and economic changes may have rendered it unnecessary or overly restrictive. Periodic examination of existing rules is thus helpful in maintaining the quality of occupational regulation. Sunset reviews also have the benefit of reviewing complaints lodged with the licensing board. These can provide important insight into the value of continuing the license. Often, the large majority of complaints are filed by other practitioners – not consumers – and are related to workers practicing without a license rather than any substantive violation of rules concerning health and safety.[110] Sunset reviews have to carefully consider what the complaint record means. In principle, few complaints could mean that licensing a particular occupation eliminates all dangerous conduct, but it can also mean that genuine consumer harms are very rare in the occupation.

To strengthen both sunset and sunrise review, it is important that the agency responsible for conducting the cost-benefit analysis is provided with adequate resources and is insulated from political interference. In addition, State legislatures might further empower the State agency in charge of conducting the review, for example, by legislating that some minimum number of votes be required to overrule the agency's recommendation. Appointing a specialized committee within the State legislature that is responsible for licensing issues may also be helpful to serve as a locus for institutional knowledge on licensing and to educate other legislators.

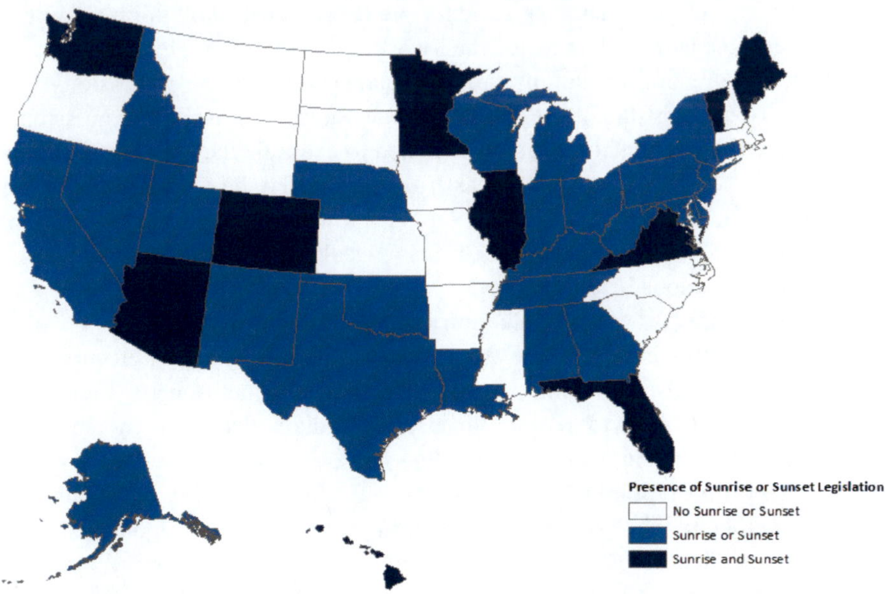


Source: Council on Licensure, Enforcement, and Regulation (2015).

Figure 13. States with Sunrise and Sunset Legislation.

Vesting responsibility for supervising licensing laws and conducting sunrise and sunset reviews in a single "umbrella agency" can be a helpful way to simultaneously ensure adequate resources, efficiency, and sufficient analytical expertise. Colorado has taken this approach in establishing its nonpartisan Department of Regulatory Agencies (DORA).[111] DORA's sunrise reviews have identified many new proposals for licensure that did not pass scrutiny, though the legislature has not always followed their recommendations.[112]

**Recent Reviews of Licensing Policy by States**

Having an established sunrise process in place is a good way to prevent future unnecessary burdens in licensing, but as licensing is already extensive in some States, reviewing current licenses systematically may be a way for States to reduce occupational licensing barriers. This has been done in several States recently with varying degrees of success.

In 2011, Michigan's Office of Regulatory Reinvention reviewed their occupational regulations using cost-benefit criteria similar to those listed in the best practices and recommended that 18 occupations, such as immigration clerical assistant and insurance solicitor, be deregulated, though only some of these were licensed.[113] The office then worked with the State legislature to try to enact these recommendations and deregulate some of these professions.[114]

The Texas Legislature created The Texas Sunset Advisory Commission, a 12-member legislative commission designed to examine the efficiency of State agencies, in 1977. In 2013, the Texas House expanded the commission's set of criteria for de-licensing an occupation. The following year, the commission reviewed the Texas Department of State Health and recommended that 6 licensed occupations be deregulated.[115]

In 2014, the Program Evaluation Division (PED) of the North Carolina General Assembly called for the establishment of a nine-member Occupational Licensing Commission, which would primarily conduct sunrise reviews of professions that wish to require licensure, mediate disagreements between occupational licensing agencies regarding jurisdictional authority, and review annual reporting requirements. Importantly, the commission would have five public members who are not licensed in an occupation regulated by an occupational licensing entity, which would reduce the number of potential conflicts of interest from members who may feel obligated to protect their occupation from scrutiny.[116]

In addition, the PED reviewed 55 occupational licensing agencies to determine if there was a continued need for licensure in these occupations.

PED scored each agency based on demonstrable impact for harm, the number of complaints and significant disciplinary actions, and the number of other States that license the occupation. The 12 lowest-scoring agencies were recommended for further review by the General Assembly.[117]

### Public Membership on Licensing Boards

Another potentially promising practice is to appoint more public members to licensing boards. Originally, licensing boards were almost exclusively populated by members of the regulated professions. Professional members often oppose public membership on the grounds that public members lack the technical expertise necessary to be an effective board member, and some States still have in place statutory requirements that governors appoint only those individuals nominated by a State professional association to serve as licensee members of a licensing board.[118]

Though members of a profession have the advantage of expertise in technical matters related to their fields, they are also more likely than public members to favor the interests of their profession over the interests of the public. For this reason, some States and nonprofits began to prioritize the inclusion of public members. California was a pioneer in this effort, achieving public member majorities on some boards as early as the 1970s, and many other States have since experimented with public members on their boards.[119] There is little reliable empirical evidence regarding the effectiveness of this reform, but anecdotal evidence suggests the value of public representation has varied greatly depending on how such members are identified and selected, whether their roles and responsibilities are made clear, and whether sufficient training and support are provided to them.[120]

## *Work to Reduce Licensing's Barriers to Mobility*

### Interstate Compacts

In a number of different areas, regulatory authorities and industry groups have moved to construct interstate compacts to further facilitate the free flow of workers. Interstate compacts may be constructed in several ways. They may be based on reciprocity agreements, with some State licenses recognized in other States. For example, many States have reciprocity agreements that allow the open practice of law by lawyers who have been admitted to the bar of another State. A different approach, taken by the Nurse Licensure Compact, is for States to construct a separate, multi-State license that installs a common set of qualifications for all compact members. States are free to maintain single-

State licensure requirements, but must consent to a separate standard that pertains to workers from other States.

In devising these agreements, States must both acknowledge and bridge the gaps that exist in their licensing requirements. This is obviously easier to do when the licensing requirements are already relatively similar across States to begin with. However, even in such circumstances, there are logistical and financial barriers to constructing a compact. For instance, States must share information about complaints against practitioners as well as potentially deal with loss of revenue from practitioners who previously paid fees in multiple States. When qualifications are substantially dissimilar across States, then some States may be concerned about the prospect of allowing other States' licensees to practice.

## RECENT SUPREME COURT DECISION ON LICENSING BOARDS AND ANTITRUST LAW

States' legal authority to license professions is well-established. In 1889, the Supreme Court in *Dent v. West Virginia* established the rights of States to license professions. Under a line of cases starting with *Parker v. Brown*, State licensing boards have been assumed to be shielded from Federal antitrust liability, in the same manner as State courts and legislatures.[1]

However, in a recent decision, *North Carolina State Board of Dental Examiners v. Federal Trade Commission*, the Supreme Court held that State licensing boards are not automatically exempted from antitrust scrutiny.[1] Under the standard articulated by the Court, if a controlling number of board members are themselves "active market participants," then the licensing board's conduct is only immune from antitrust scrutiny if it is (1) clearly articulated State policy, and (2) actively supervised by the State.

The extent to which the Court's decision will in practice increase State licensing boards' exposure to antitrust actions and constrain occupational regulation is unclear. However, States may respond to the Court's decision by increasing their supervision requirements or by reconstituting the membership of the boards to include more public members, for example.

One danger is that when States are harmonizing their licensing requirements or creating an interstate compact, they may settle on a level of licensing that is inappropriately stringent or may favor the lowest common denominator. For example, regulators may decide to bar all workers with criminal records from obtaining a license or participating in the compact, even when the criminal record is not specifically relevant to practice in an occupation. In general, States should avoid simply adopting the licensing requirements of the most stringent States. However, if States with more stringent requirements will not agree to accept workers from other States, then States should consider adopting a "two-tiered" structure that allows States with more flexible requirements to retain their rules while restricting interstate reciprocity to workers who satisfy a higher bar. Such agreements also should avoid creating a "race to the bottom" and instead seek to strike the appropriate balance in establishing requirements.

***Federal Reform Efforts***

Licensing reform takes place at the State level, but Federal resources can help to incentivize State collaboration and expand resources for States to use when making their own reforms. The President's FY2016 Budget includes $15 million in new discretionary funding at the Department of Labor to identify, explore, and address areas where licensing requirements create barriers to labor market entry or labor mobility. The first round of grants would fund a consortium of States, managed by an intermediary or leading State, to conduct analyses of licensing requirements and develop ways to make licenses portable across States, including cross-State licensing reciprocity agreements to accept each other's licenses. The Department would use a portion of the funding for research to identify measurable criteria that identify occupations for which licensing is not justified.

This research would inform the second round of grants that will fund individual States that are working to reduce licensing barriers, as appropriate, and support their work in reviewing whether State licensing requirements should be modified, as well as developing voluntary certification and credentialing frameworks to replace unnecessary licensing. Grants could also provide resources to States to build coalitions across education, business, and consumer groups to reduce licensing burdens.

As described previously, the Federal government has also called on States to make reforms that benefit military spouses and veterans. The frequent interstate movement of military families presents a particular hardship for civilian spouses who must continually seek new employment.

## THE NURSE LICENSURE COMPACT

Introduced in the United States in 2000, the Nurse Licensure Compact (NLC) aims to lower barriers to geographic mobility for licensed practical nurses, vocational nurses, and registered nurses. As of March 2015, 25 States participate in the Compact.[1] The NLC uses a system of "mutual recognition," in which an RN or a LPN/VN located in a State that has adopted the NLC may acquire a single multi-State license that allows them to practice—either electronically or in person—in any other State that has adopted the NLC. Nurses are still required to obtain a new license after a permanent move. DePasquale and Stange (2014) find that NLC adoption does increase the probability of interstate commuting among nurses.[1]

The NLC illustrates the challenges of coming to agreement across States with different standards. A key difficulty in forming the NLC was the variation across States in whether and how workers with criminal histories were licensed. While individual States are free to set their licensing requirements as they see fit (for instance, by allowing nurses with criminal records to apply), the multi-State license is currently only available to nurses who satisfy a more restrictive standard (nurses with felony convictions may not apply). Ideally, the Compact would use a more finely-tuned approach that accounted for details of workers' criminal records, including their relevance and how recent they are, and this approach would extend to the multi-State license. (For example, a separate compact under development for physical therapy will not categorically exclude workers with felony convictions.) But when States fail to reach agreement, a two- tiered system is preferable to achieving no reciprocity at all.

Compounding this difficulty is the necessity of becoming licensed in each new State. If licensing burdens are high enough, then military spouses may be deterred from participating in the labor market altogether.

Following publication of a joint Treasury and Defense Department report in early 2012, many States passed legislation to enhance reciprocity for spouses of active military service members. Expediting the application process and providing temporary licenses, as the Treasury/Defense report recommended, will help military spouses working in a licensed occupation to more easily transition to a new State and remain part of the labor force.[121]

Relatedly, the Joining Forces initiative has worked to help veterans transition to civilian employment. Frequently, service members develop skills relevant to civilian occupations that nonetheless do not conform to the typical pattern (e.g., classroom instruction, internship, etc.) Showing licensing authorities that veterans have obtained relevant skills and establishing competency-based pathways to licensure are vital to re-integrating veterans into the civilian labor market.

## CONCLUSION

In many fields, occupational licensing plays an important role in protecting consumers and ensuring quality. Licensing can also encourage practitioners to invest in and maintain their skills. These benefits are important to both consumers and licensed practitioners. However, as detailed in this report, the practice of licensing can impose substantial costs on job seekers, consumers, and the economy more generally. This is particularly true when licensing regulations are poorly aligned toward consumer protection and when they are not updated to reflect a changing economy. This report informs future discussions of these costs and benefits by providing a thorough overview of the research on licensing, as well as a picture of how licensing has expanded within a changing economy. It also identifies several potential reforms that would help to ease burdens on workers and consumers, while still ensuring quality and protecting the public. In doing so, it builds on the Obama Administration's goals of promoting the most innovative and effective, and least burdensome, tools to achieve regulatory ends.[122]

Yet there is more work to be done. Congress and the Federal government should do their part by providing information and resources to policymakers, and identifying ways to optimize Federal licensing requirements. Researchers must continue to assess and identify promising policy reforms. Ultimately, however, most of the power is in the hands of the States. State legislators and policymakers should adopt institutional reforms that promote a more careful and individualized approach to occupational regulation that takes into account its costs and benefits, and harmonizes requirements across States. If they are successful, the collective effect of their efforts could be substantial: making it easier for qualified workers to find jobs and move where they choose, increasing access to essential goods and services, and lessening heavy burdens on certain populations, such as military families, immigrants, and individuals with criminal records.

Instituting a more rational approach to occupational regulation would improve economic opportunity and allow American workers to take advantage of new developments in today's economy.

## Resources for Policymakers on Licensing Reform

There are a number of resources available online that can provide information to policymakers working to reform occupational licensing.

You can find out which States require sunrise or sunset audits on the Council on Licensure, Enforcement & Regulation's (CLEAR) *"Sunrise, Sunset and State Agency Audits"* page. You can also view each state's published *sunrise, sunset, and performance audit reports.*

To find specific occupational regulation statutes by State, use the *"Occupational Regulation Statutes"* page on CLEAR's website.

Legislators questioning whether or not an occupation should be licensed can refer to, *"Questions A Legislat or Should Ask,"* written by CLEAR, which includes detailed considerations to take into account.

If you want to look at occupational regulation in other nations for comparison, CLEAR has a *"Regulat ory Models"* page with summaries of the regulatory models of Canada, Mexico, and the United Kingdom.

The Department of Labor sponsors an *online database* in which one can search by occupation, license name, or licensing agency to see the occupational regulation requirements in different States.

The *National Inventory of Collateral Consequences of Conviction* is an interactive tool that allows users to see what automatic penalties, disabilities, or disadvantages (collateral consequences) are imposed on a person who has committed a crime in a specific State. Policymakers can use this tool to see how a conviction will affect someone's long-term ability to work in a regulated occupation in their area.

If you have additional questions about the subject matter of this report, please contact the *Office of Economic Policy* at the U.S. Department of the Treasury.

# V. RESEARCH APPENDIX

## Impacts on Quality, Health, and Safety

A wide range of studies have examined the question of whether licensing improves the quality of goods and services, as would be the case if licensing successfully limited the practice of an occupation to high-quality practitioners. The studies we reviewed on quality, health and safety are summarized in Research Appendix Table 1. Overall, the empirical research does not find large improvements in quality or health and safety from more stringent licensing. In fact, in only two out of the 12 studies was greater licensing associated with quality improvements.

**Research Appendix Table 1. Studies on the Effects of Licensing on Quality, Health, and Safety**

| Paper | Licensed Occupation | Type of Licensing Restriction Studied | Measurement of Quality/Health/Safety | Impact |
|---|---|---|---|---|
| Larsen (2015) | Teaching | Stricter licensing requirements in high-income districts | Student test scores and teacher qualifications | Increase in quality in both measures |
| Larsen (2015) | Teaching | Stricter licensing requirements in low-income districts | Student test scores and teacher qualifications | No effect |
| Kane, Rockoff, and Staiger (2008) | Teaching | Licensing versus alternative certification or no license | Student test scores | No effect |
| Angrist and Guryan (2007) | Teaching | Mandated teacher testing to obtain license | Teacher educational background | No effect |
| Kane and Staiger (2005) | Teaching | Certification requirement | Student test scores | No effect |
| Kleiner and Petree (1988) | Teaching | Stricter licensing requirements | Student test scores | Unclear effect |
| Powell and Vorotnikov (2012) | Real estate | Continuing education component | Complaints to the real estate licensing board | No effect |
| Kleiner and Kudrle (2000) | Dentistry | Tighter requirements | Dental health (dental deterioration and amount of repair needed) | No effect |
| Holen (1978) | Dentistry | Stringency of entry requirements | Adverse outcomes such as cavities and broken or chipped teeth; general dental health | Increase in quality |
| Klee (2013) | Legal, Accounting, Cosmetology, Teaching | Stricter licensing requirements | Vocational training enrollment | No effect or modest increase in quality |
| Carpenter (2012) | Floristry | Licensing requirement | Rating of floral arrangement by florist-judges | No effect |
| Healey (1973) | Lab technicians | Restrictions on assistance in clinical labs | Quality of output (as measured by proficiency testing) | No effect |
| Maurizi (1980) | Building Contracting | Increases in number of schools offering courses to help contractors pass their exam (proxy for higher pass rate) | Consumer complaints about licensees | Modest reduction in quality |

The variety of occupations, range of quality and outcome measures, and duration over which this subject has been studied are apparent from scanning the rows of the table. Most empirical evidence does not find that stricter licensing requirements improve quality, public safety or health. While older research suggests that more stringent entry requirements are associated with lower rates of untreated dental disease,[123] more recent studies that control for potentially confounding factors find no evidence that tighter dentistry licensing requirements lead to better dental health, though they do lead to higher prices.[124] Studying quality in a newly-licensed area, floral design, Carpenter (2012) recruited a randomly selected sample of florist-judges to compare floral arrangements produced by licensed retail florists from Louisiana and unlicensed florists from Texas. He found that licensing appears not to result in a statistically significant difference in the quality of floral arrangements.[125] Other research finds that imposing licensing requirements or stricter regulations (such as performance examinations or education requirements) did not significantly affect the severity of injuries suffered among electricians.[126]

Other research suggests that licensing is not always adequate to address quality concerns, but may be complementary with other forms of regulation. For example, Phelan (1974) distributed televisions with known defects in areas with and without licensing requirements for television repair workers. He found that fraud was not lower in areas with licensing alone, but was lower when licensing was coupled with a State agency that investigated fraud allegations.[127]

Much research on the impact of licensing restrictions on quality and public safety focuses on the impact of scope of practice restrictions (laws limiting the range of services that some practitioners can legally provide). There is evidence that Advanced Practice Registered Nurses can provide a range of primary care services to patients at least as effectively as physicians, including wellness and prevention services, diagnosis and management of uncomplicated acute conditions, and management of chronic diseases.[128] A systematic review of the literature found that outcomes for nurse practitioners (NPs) compared to physicians (or teams without NPs) are comparable or better for all 11 outcomes reviewed, including blood glucose, blood pressure, mortality, patient satisfaction with care, and number of emergency department visits.[129]

One important channel through which licensing might affect quality is through increasing the training of licensed practitioners. Data on accountants, attorneys, cosmetologists, and teachers suggests that while stricter licensing requirements are not associated with higher rates of vocational class enrollment, such restrictions are associated with additional training since workers began their most recent job.[130] One possible explanation for the latter finding is that many States require licensed workers to accumulate work experience before they become licensed.

However, occupational licensing requirements vary considerably across States and occupations, and most of the empirical evidence on licensing comes from looking at very specific examples. While the aforementioned studies indicate that occupational licensing does not guarantee quality improvements, they likewise do not indicate that all licensing frameworks fail to increase service quality.

## Impact on Prices

While quality can be defined in many ways and is often difficult to measure, the evidence on licensing's effects on prices is unequivocal: many studies find that more restrictive licensing laws lead to higher prices for consumers. As before, we summarize the studies we've reviewed in the table below. In 9 of the 11 studies we reviewed, significantly higher prices accompanied stricter licensing. In addition to the studies listed below, Kleiner and Todd (2009) find that two particular mortgage broker licensing requirements, financial bonding and minimum net worth requirements, are associated with a higher percentage of high-priced loans originated and lower volumes of loans processed, but that overall indices of the tightness of mortgage broker licensing are not significantly associated with market outcomes.[131]

## Impact on Employment and Wages

While credibly estimating employment effects is difficult given available data, there is some evidence indicating that licensing directly restricts the supply of workers in licensed professions. Kleiner (2006) examines three professions that are licensed in some States but not in others, and finds that employment growth was higher in the unlicensed States relative to the licensed ones from 1990 to 2000. He also compares employment growth rates in several occupations that have different levels of licensing (licensed in all

States, licensed in some States, and not licensed in any States), and there too finds that licensing is associated with slower employment growth.[132]

Federman et al. (2006) find that State licensing laws that require English proficiency or greater training suppress the number of Vietnamese-American manicurists, as well as the overall number of manicurists.[133] Similarly, Cathles et al. (2010) find that licensing laws which require funeral directors to also be embalmers reduce the proportion of female funeral directors, and that the overall number of funeral directors per capita is lower on average in States that have these laws.[134]

As previously referenced, research finds that States with the least restrictive regulations of nurse practitioners (NPs) had more licensed NPs and that patients in these States were 2.5 times more likely to receive their primary care from NPs than the most restrictive States. Other factors, such as demographic variables and the availability of primary care physicians and physician assistants, may partly explain this variation. However, when these factors were controlled for, States' degree of regulation explained 16.8 percent of the State variation in NP care.[135] In addition, other research finds that State licensing laws requiring that electricians pass an oral examination or meet experience requirements were associated with fewer per capita electricians.[136] However, research on the Nurse Licensure Compact, which was designed to ease licensure portability among nurses but not reduce overall licensing requirements at the State level, showed no effect of the Compact on nurses' employment or labor force participation.[137]

As described in Section I, the effect of restricting entry to licensed occupations has proved easier to study in terms of wages: restrictions are expected to raise the wages of those who manage to enter licensed occupations, and lower the wages of other workers, leading to a wage gap.[138]

Basic empirical evidence points clearly to a wage gap between licensed and unlicensed workers, though this research provides little insight as to how much of the gap is attributable to wage gains for licensed workers and how much is attributable to wage losses for workers who are shut out of the sector.[139] For example, research finds that certain licensing provisions increase barbers' earnings by between 11 and 22 percent relative to unlicensed workers with similar education, and that massage therapists working in States with licensing receive an earnings premium of as much as 16 percent compared to massage therapists in States without licensing.[140] Kleiner and Krueger (2013) note that most of the estimates of cross-sectional studies of licensing on wages find that licensing results in 10 percent to 15 percent higher wages for licensed workers relative to unlicensed workers with similar characteristics.[141] Using their Westat survey, Kleiner and Krueger (2013) find that licensing at the State level confers a wage premium of around 17 percent, whereas the combination of State and either Federal or local licensing has an estimate effect of around 25 percent. Local licenses by themselves are not associated with higher wages, and certification has a much smaller effect on wages.[142]

However, because licensed workers generally have more training than unlicensed workers, and because they may differ in other important ways, these wage gaps may reflect educational or other differences across workers. More careful estimates of the wage gap between licensed and unlicensed workers try to account for these differences in one of two ways. First, they may compare workers *within* licensed occupations. Many occupations are licensed in some States but not others. Also, States may only require that only some workers in a field be licensed, such as architects who sign off on plans, but not other workers who perform similar tasks, such as sketchers, modelers, or construction managers. By comparing licensed and unlicensed workers who perform very similar work functions, researchers may get a better picture of the true wage benefits from licensing per se.[143] Second, researchers can sometimes observe wages for workers as they transition in or out of a licensed occupation. By comparing earnings for the same worker both with and without a license, researchers know that any fixed characteristic of the worker cannot explain the earnings changes. Again, this can give them more confidence that they have isolated the impact of a license per se, rather than the impact of being one kind of worker and not another.

Using these methods, the wage premium from licensing is more modest, and is often estimated as zero. Gittleman, Kleiner and Klee (2015) find that workers with a license earn around 8.4 percent higher wages on average controlling for detailed occupation.[144] Researchers have also examined the earnings of workers who switched from unlicensed to licensed occupations (and vice versa). Gittleman and Kleiner (2013) found that moving to a licensed occupation from an unlicensed occupation conferred no wage gain. When they control for occupations using broad occupational controls, they find that licensing has an effect of around 8 percent. However, this effect disappears when they use more detailed controls.[145] Klee (2013) discovers limited evidence of a licensing wage premium, and even finds that in some cases more stringent licensing regulations are actually associated with a wage discount.[146]

**Research Appendix Table 2. Studies on the Price Effects of Licensing**

| Paper | Licensed Occupation | Type of Licensing Restriction Studied | Type of Price Studied | Percent Impact |
|---|---|---|---|---|
| Kleiner et al. (2014) | Nursing | Medium level of regulation | Price of well-child medical exams | 6.0 |
| Kleiner et al. (2014) | Nursing | High level of regulation | Price of well-child medical exams | 16.0 |
| Kleiner and Todd (2009) | Mortgage Brokers | An additional $100,000 in state broker bonding/net worth requirement | Probability that a mortgage is high-priced | 5.4pp |
| Kleiner and Todd (2009) | Mortgage Brokers | Index of other state broker licensing requirements | Probability that a mortgage is high-priced | No effect |
| Kleiner and Kudrle (2000) | Dentistry | Pass rate of dental exam | Price of filling a cavity | -1.0 |
| Kleiner and Kudrle (2000) | Dentistry | High level of regulation (no reciprocity or endorsement) | Price of filling a cavity | 11.0 |
| Kleiner and Kudrle (2000) | Dentistry | Restriction index based on regulation and pass rate levels relative to average | Price of filling a cavity | No effect |
| Liang and Ogur (1987) | Dentistry | Restrictions on number of hygienists and assistants or their functions | Price of dental visit in 1970 | 5.0 |
| Liang and Ogur (1987) | Dentistry | Restrictions on number of hygienists and assistants or their functions | Price of dental visit in 1982 | 7.0 |
| Conrad and Sheldon (1982) | Dentistry | Limited reciprocity | Price index of dental services | 3.3 |
| Conrad and Sheldon (1982) | Dentistry | Restrictions on the number of branch offices | Price index of services | 4.0 |
| Conrad and Sheldon (1982) | Dentistry | Restrictions on the number of hygienists | Price index of services | 4.0 |
| Shepard (1978) | Dentistry | No reciprocity (ability to have one state's license recognized by another state) | Prices of 12 different dental services | Ranges from -0.2 to 17.9, average of 6.5 |

Moreover, not all licensed occupations experience the same wage boosts. The figure below shows the difference in hourly earnings between licensed and unlicensed workers by occupation. Wage premia are highest in some of the occupations that have the greatest proportions of licensed workers, such as health care support and practice, education, and legal occupations. In these occupations, unlicensed workers are rare and for that reason are likely to be quite different from the licensed workers who dominate the profession. However, even in occupations with large numbers of both licensed and unlicensed workers – like installation and repair, sales, and grounds keeping – licensed workers still earn 5 to 10 percent higher wages.[147]

## Impact on Geographic Mobility

Since many occupations are licensed at the State level, licensed practitioners typically have to acquire a new license when they move across

States. This alone entails various procedural hurdles, such as paying fees, filling out administrative paperwork, and submitting an application and waiting for it to be processed. Moreover, since each State sets its own licensing requirements, these often vary across State lines, and licensed individuals seeking to move to another State often discover that they must meet new qualifications (such as education, experience, training, testing, etc.) if they want to continue working in their occupation. The resulting costs in both time and money can discourage people from moving. This system is especially burdensome for some populations, such as military spouses, who are very likely to move across State lines.[148] Diminished mobility generates inefficiency in the labor market, with workers unable to migrate easily to the jobs in which they are most productive. In times of economic distress, this reduced mobility would be especially harmful, as workers would have a difficult time leaving– or for some practitioners, delivering services to – hard-hit areas.

As described in Section I, there has been relatively little research on the impact of State licensing on interstate mobility. In addition to the research described in Section I, other research examines the impacts of the Nurse Licensure Compact (NLC), an interstate compact that allows registered nurses and licensed practical and vocational nurses to practice across State lines in participating States without acquiring a new license. The authors find modest positive effects of NLC adoption on travel time to work (which indicates more mobility) and likelihood of working across State lines, especially among nurses living close to State borders.[149] There is reason to think that this estimate may understate the impact of State restrictions on mobility, given that the NLC did not fully eliminate barriers to licensure portability in participating States.[150]

Several older studies also find that more restrictive licensing depresses mobility.[151] Although these studies employ more limited statistical techniques, they make an effort to allow for the fact that different types of people choose licensed occupations over unlicensed ones, and therefore it is uninformative to simply compare mobility between licensed and unlicensed occupations without accounting for other workers differences.

To add to this literature, we have carried out our own analysis using both the Survey of Income and Program Participation (SIPP) and the American Community Survey (ACS). We first compare the interstate mobility of licensed and unlicensed workers in the SIPP. To account for the facts that licensed workers are typically more educated than unlicensed workers, and more educated workers are more mobile, we compare the interstate mobility of licensed workers and certified workers. Certified workers are likely comparable to licensed workers, yet they can often take their certification with them across State lines.

Over the eight-month period starting in late 2012, licensed workers were about 20 percent less likely and certified workers in the SIPP were about 60 percent more likely than non-licensed, non- certified workers to change States. These patterns are broadly similar when we control for available demographic variables, suggesting that licensing may indeed limit interstate mobility when compared to similar workers who hold certifications.[152]

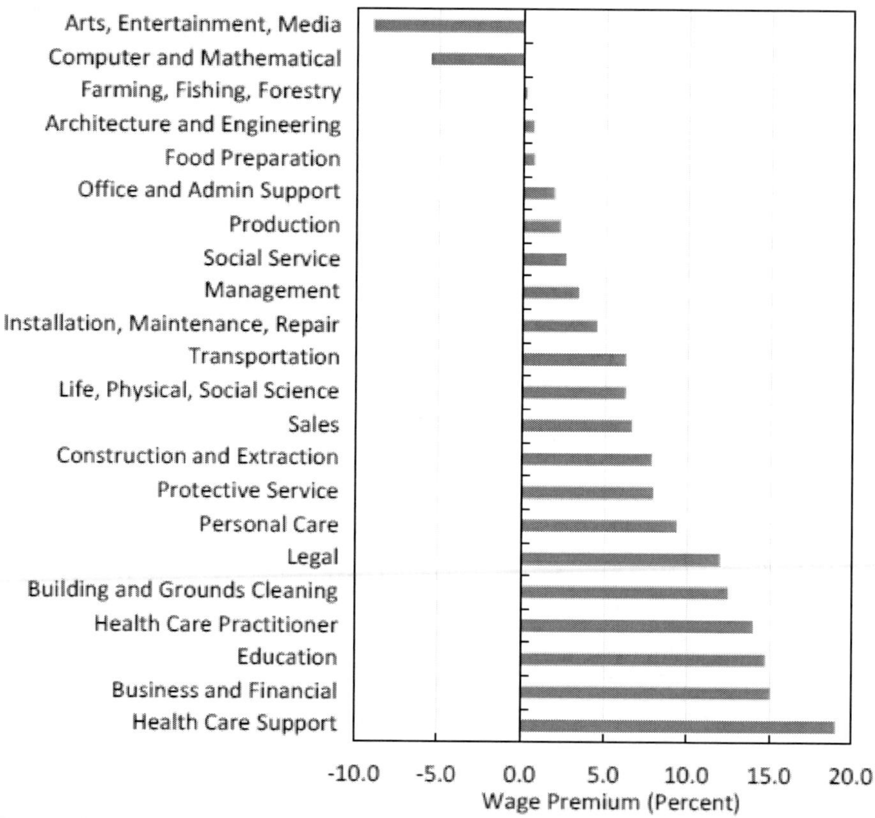


Source: Survey of Income and Program Participation 2008 Panel; UST calculations.

Research Appendix Figure 1. Wage Effect of Licensing by Occupation.

Using the ACS, we compare the likelihood of moving over longer versus shorter distances for workers in licensed occupations to those in unlicensed occupations. This is an alternative test to that in the SIPP. If the need to re-license poses a barrier to mobility, then the biggest differences between workers in licensed and unlicensed occupations should show up for moves that require a change of license. As discussed already, licensing predominantly occurs at the State-level, so moves across State lines would be more difficult for workers in licensed occupations than those in other occupations if licensing posed a true barrier. On the other hand, if the type of person who enters licensed work is simply less likely to move than individuals who go into other lines of work, then licensed workers should be less likely to move than other workers regardless of distance. Our analysis is similar to forthcoming work by Kleiner and Johnson.

As shown in Figure 1 in Section I, there are substantial differences in the likelihood of moving across State lines between workers in licensed occupations versus other workers, while there are only modest differences between the two groups in the likelihood of moving within a State. The figure shows that interstate migration rates for workers in the most licensed occupations are lower by an amount equal to nearly 15 percent of the average migration rate compared to those in the least licensed occupations. But the difference between these workers in within-State migration is much smaller, only about 3 percent of the average rate. These impacts are also much larger for younger licensed workers: this difference is 21 percent of the average interstate migration rate for those under 35 compared to an impact of about 12 percent for workers over 35.

## REFERENCES

11 U.S. Code § 523 - Exceptions to discharge.

Alabama Administrative Code r. 330-X-3-.01.

Allen, Elaine and Jeff Seaman. (2014). "Grade Change: Tracking Online Education in the United States." *Babson Survey Research Group*. http://www.onlinelearningsurvey.com/reports/gradechange.pdf.

Alexander, J. Trent, Sarah Flood, Katie Genadek, Miriam King, Steven Ruggles, Matthew B. Schroeder, & Brandon Trample. (2010). Integrated Public Use Microdata Series, Current Population Survey: Version 3.0. [Machine-readable database]

Akerlof, George A. (1970). "The Market for Lemons: Quality Uncertainty and the Market Mechanism." *Quarterly Journal of Economics*, 84, no. 3, 488-500.

Ambrogi, Robert. 2015. "Who Says you Need a Law Degree to Practice Law?" *Washington Post.* http:// www.washingtonpost.com/ opinions/ closing-the-justice-gap/2015/03/13/a5f576c8-c754-11e4-aa1a-86135599 fb0f_story.html.

American Association of Nurse Practitioners. (2015). "2015 Nurse Practitioner State Practice Environment." http://www.aanp.org/images/ documents/ State-leg- reg/stateregulatorymap.pdf.

American Bar Association National Inventory of Collateral Consequences of Conviction. http://www.abacollateralconsequences.org/search/.

American Nurses Association. (2013). "Nurse Licensure Compact." http:// www.nursingworld.org/MainMenuCategories/Policy-Advocacy/State/ Legislative-Agenda-Reports/LicensureCompact/INLC-TalkingPoints.pdf.

American Physical Therapy Association. (2012). "APTA to Explore Feasibility of Transitioning PTA Education toBachelor Degree Level." http://www.apta.org/PTinMotion/NewsNow/2012/6/15/HODRC2/.

American Speech-Language-Hearing Association."StateTelepractice Requirements."http://www.asha.org/Advocacy/state/State-Telepractice-Requirements/.

Arkansas House Bill (1158). http:// www.arkansashouse.org/ bills? bill= 2015RHB1158.

Arrow, Kenneth J. (1963). "Uncertainty and the Welfare Economics of Medical Care. 1963.." *American Economic Review*, 53, no. 5: 941–969.

Arrow, Kenneth J. (1971). "Essays in the Theory of Risk-Bearing." Chicago, IL: Markham Publishing Co.

Baker, Dean. (2014). "Doctors and Drugs: Promoting Growth and Equality through Free Trade." *Cato Online Forum.* http:// www.cato.org/ publications/cato-online-forum/doctors-drugs-promoting-growth-equality-through-free-trade.

Barnes, Linda L. (2003). "The Acupuncture Wars: The Professionalizing of American Acupuncture—A View from Massachusetts." *Medical Anthropology* 22, no. 3, 261-301.

Beck, Allen J. (2006). "The Importance of Successful Reentry to Jail Population Growth." Presented at *the Urban Institute's Jail Reentry Roundtable.* http:// www.urban.org/ sites/ default/files/beck.ppt.

Bernal v. Fainter, 467 U.S. 216. 1984.

Blanchard, Olivier. & Lawrence, Katz. (1992). "Regional Evolutions." *Brookings Papers on Economic Activity*, no. 1, 1-75.

Brinegar, Pamela L. & Kara L, Schmitt. (1992). "State Occupational and Professional Licensure." *The Book of the States*, 567–80. Lexington, KY: Council of State Governments.

Brown, Jennifer. & John, Morgan. (2006). "Reputation in Online Auctions: The Market for Trust." *California Management Review* 49, no. 1, 61-81.

Bureau of Justice Statistics. (2012). "Survey of State Criminal History Information Systems, 2012." U.S. Department of Justice. https:// www.ncjrs.gov/pdffiles1/bjs/grants/244563.pdf. California Business and Professions Code § 3057. http://optometry.ca.gov/formspubs/endorsement.pdf.

Cairo, Isabel. (2013). "The Slowdown in Business Employment Dynamics: The Role of Changing Skill Demands." Job Market Paper. http:// www.econ. upf.edu/gpefm/jm/pdf/paper/JMP%20Cairo.pdf.

Calvo-Friedman, Jennesa. (2014). "The Uncertain Terrain of State Occupational Licensing Laws for Noncitizens: A Preemption Analysis." *Georgetown Law Journal*, 102, no. 5, 1597-1645.

Carpenter II, Dick M. (2012). "Testing the Utility of Licensing: Evidence from a Field Experiment on Occupational Regulation." *Journal of Applied Business and Economics*, 13, no. 2: 28-41. Carpenter, Dick, Angela C. Erickson, Lisa Knepper, and John K. Ross. 2012. "License to Work: A National Study of Burdens from Occupational Licensing." Institute for Justice. https://www.ij.org/licensetowork.

Carroll, Sidney L. & Robert J, Gaston. (1981). "Occupational Restrictions and the Quality of Service Received: Some Evidence." *Southern Economic Journal*, 47, no. 4, 959-976.

Carson, E. Ann. & William, J. Sabol. (2012). "Prisoners in 2011." U.S. Department of Justice, Bureau of Justice Statistics. http:// www.bjs.gov/content/pub/pdf/p11.pdf.

Cassidy, Amanda. (2012). "Health Policy Brief: Nurse Practitioners and Primary Care." *Health Affairs*, 1-4.

Cathles, Alison, David E. Harrington, & Kathy Krynski. (2010). "The Gender Gap in Funeral Directors: Burying Women with Ready-to-Embalm Laws?" *British Journal of Industrial Relations*, *48*, no. 4, 688-705.

Chaudhry, Humayun J., Lisa A. Robin, Eric M. Fish, Donald H. Polk, & Daniel Gifford, J. (2015). "Improving Access and Mobility – The

Interstate Medical Licensure Compact." *The New England Journal of Medicine*, *372*, no. 17, 1581-1583.

Citizen Advocacy Center. (1995). *Public Representation on HealthCare Regulatory, Governing, and Oversight Bodies: Strategies for Success.*

Colorado's Department of Regulatory Agencies. Interview by National Economic Council. 2015. Washington, DC.

Connecticut Department of Public Health. 2015. *Scope of Practice Requests for 2014 – 2015.* http:// www.ct.gov/ dph/cwp/ view.asp?a =3121&Q= 56 3950&PM=1.

Connecticut General Assembly. (2009). "Scope of Practice Determination for Health Care Professions." Legislative Program Review and Investigations Committee.http://www.cga.ct.gov/2009/pridata/Studies/PDF/Scope_of_Practice_Final_Report.PDF.

Council of Economic Advisers. (2015). *The Economic Report of the President.*

Council on Licensure Enforcement and Regulation. *Sunrise, Sunset and State Agency Audits.* http://www.clearhq.org/page-486181.

Cowen, Tyler & Alex Tabarrok. (2015). "The End of Asymmetric Information." *Cato Unbound.* http://www.cato-unbound.org/ 2015/ 04/ 06/ alex-tabarrok-tyler-cowen/end-asymmetric-information.

Cox, Carolyn. & Susan, Foster. (1990). "The Costs and Benefits of Occupational Regulation." Federal Trade Commission. https:// www. ftc. gov/system/files/documents/reports/costs-benefits-occupational-regulation/cox_foster_-_occupational_licensing.pdf.

Craddock, Larry. (2008). "'Good Moral Character' as a Licensing Standard." *Journal of the National Association of Administrative Law Judiciary*, 28, no. 2, 450-469.

Davis, Steven J. & John, Haltiwanger. (2014). "Labor Market Fluidity and Economic Performance." NBER Working Paper 20479.

Dent v. State of West Virginia, 129 U.S. 114. 1889.

Department of Defense and States, Partnering to Support Military Families. "Removing Licensure Impediments for Transitioning Military Spouses." http://www.usa4militaryfamilies.dod.mil/MOS/f?p=USA4:ISSUE:0::::P2_ISSUE:2

DePasquale, Christina, and Kevin Stange. (2014). "State Regulation and the Mobility of Nurses: An Examination of the Nurse Licensure Compact." Emory University Working Paper 14-14. http:// economics.emory.edu/ home/documents/workingpapers/depasquale_14_14_pap er.pdf.

Edlin, Aaron. & Rebecca, Haw. (2014). "Cartels by Another Name: Should Licensed Occupations Face Antitrust Scrutiny?" *University of Pennsylvania Law Review*, *162*, 1093-1164.

Eibner, Christine E., Peter, S., Hussey, M., Susan, Ridgely. & Elizabeth A., McGlynn. (2009). "Controlling Health Care Spending in Massachusetts: An Analysis of Options." *RAND Health*. http:// pulse.ncpolicywatch.org/ wp- content/uploads/2010/02/mass_cost_control.pdf.

Executive Order 13563. (January 18, 2011). *Federal Register*, *76*(14).

Fairman, Julie A., Susan Hassmiller, John W. Rowe, & Donna E. Shalala. (2011). "Broadening the Scope of Nursing Practice." *The New England Journal of Medicine*, *364*, no. 3, 193-196.

Federman, Maya N., David E. Harrington. & Kathy J. Krynski. (2006). "The Impact of State Licensing Regulations on Low-Skilled Immigrants: The Case of Vietnamese Manicurists." *American Economic Review*, *96*, no. 2, 237-241.

Freed, Gary L., Kelly M. Dunham, & Acham, Gebremariam. (2013). "Changes in Hospitals' Credentialing Requirements for Board Certification from 2005 to 2010." *Journal of Hospital Medicine*, *8*, no. 6, 298-303.

Friedman, Milton. (1962). "Capitalism and Freedom." Chicago, IL: The University of Chicago Press. Friedman, Milton and Simon Kuznets. 1954. "Income from Independent Professional Practice." New York, NY: NBER.

Gellhorn, Walter. (1976). "The Abuse of Occupational Licensing." *The University of Chicago Law Review*, *44*, no. 1, 6-27.

Gittleman, Maury., Mark, A. Klee. & Morris, M. Kleiner. (2015). "Analyzing the Labor Market Outcomes of Occupational Licensing." NBER Working Paper 20961.

Gittleman, Maury. & Morris, M. Kleiner. (2013). "Wage Effects of Unionization and Occupational Licensing Coverage in the United States." NBER Working Paper 19061.

Greene, Karen. (1969). "Occupational Licensing and the Supply of Nonprofessional Manpower." Washington, DC: Manpower Administration, U.S. Department of Labor.

Hadfield, Gillian K. (2014). "The Cost of Law: Promoting Access to Justice through the (Un)Corporate Practice of Law." *International Review of Law and Economics*, *38*, 43-63.

Hall, Matthew., Audrey, Singer., Gordon, F., De, Jong. & Deborah, Roempke Graefe. (2011). "The Geography of Immigrant Skills:

Educational Profiles of Metropolitan Areas." *State of Metropolitan America*, no. *33*. TheBrookings Institution. http:// www. brookings.edu/~/ media/research/files/papers/2011/6/immigrants-singer/06_immigrants_ singer.pdf.

Health Resources and Services Administration. (2014). "Shortage Designation: Health Professional Shortage Areas and Medically Underserved Areas/Populations." U.S. Department of Health and Human Services. http://www.hrsa.gov/shortage/.

Holderness, Richard A., Stephen, G. Valker. & Stephen, D. Butler. "State-By-State Guide to Architect, Engineer, and Contractor Licensing." Aspen Publishers Online, 1995.

Holen, Arlene S. (1965). "Effects of Professional Licensing Arrangements on Interstate Labor Mobility and Resource Allocation." *Journal of Political Economy*, *73*, no. 5, 492-498.

Holen, Arlene. (1978). "The Economics of Dental Licensing." Department of Health, Education and Welfare.

Iglehart, John K. (2013). "Expanding the Role of Advanced Nurse Practitioners—Risks and Rewards." *The New England Journal of Medicine*, *368*, no. 20, 1935-1941. In re Griffiths, 413 U.S. 717. 1973.

Indiana General Assembly. (2015). House Bill 1303. https:// iga.in.gov/ legislative/2015/bills/house/1303.

Institute of Education Sciences. (2015). *The Condition of Education 2015*. U.S. Department of Education. http://nces.ed.gov/pubs2015/2015144.pdf.

Institute of Medicine of the National Academies. (2010). "The Future of Nursing: Focus on Scope ofPractice." http:// www.iom.edu/ Reports/ 2010/The-Future-of-Nursing-Leading-Change-Advancing-Health/Report-Brief-Scope-of-Practice.aspx.

Iowa, Legislature. (2015). House File 196. http://coolice.legis.iowa.gov/Cool-ICE/default.asp?Category=billinfo&Service=Billbook&menu=false&hbill =HF196.

Iraq and Afghanistan Veterans of America and Prudential Financial, Inc. (2012). *Veterans' Employment Challenges: Perceptions and Experiences of Transitioning from Military to Civilian Life*. http:// www. prudential. com/documents/public/VeteransEmploymentChallenges.pdf.

Johnson, Janna E. & Morris, M. Kleiner. (2015). "Is Occupational Licensing a Barrier to Interstate Migration?" Forthcoming.

Judicial Council of California. (2004). *Statewide Action Plan for Serving Self-Represented Litigants*. http://www.courts.ca.gov/documents/selfreplits rept.pdf.

Klee, Mark A. (2013). "How Do Professional Licensing Regulations Affect Practitioners? New Evidence." U.S. Bureau of Labor Statistics, SEHSD Working Paper 2013-30.

Klein, Linda. (2010). *Report on the Survey of Judges on the Impact of the Economic Downturn on Representation in theCourts*.ABA Coalition for Justice.http://www.americanbar.org/content/dam/aba/migrated/JusticeCenter/PublicDocume nts/CoalitionforJusticeSurveyReport.authcheckdam.pdf.

Kleiner, Morris M. (1990). "Are There Economic Rents for More Restrictive Occupational Licensing Practices?' *42nd Annual Proceedings. United States: Industrial Relations Research Association*, 177-185.

Kleiner, Morris M. (2000). "Occupational Licensing." *Journal of Economic Perspectives*, 14, no. 4, 189-202. American Economic Association.

Kleiner, Morris M. (2006). "Licensing Occupations: Ensuring Quality or Restriction Competition?" *W.E. Upjohn Institute for Employment Research* 1-15. Kalamazoo, MI: Upjohn Institute Press. http:// dx.doi.org/ 10.17848/9781429454865.

Kleiner, Morris M. *Guild-Ridden Labor Markets: The Curious Case of Occupational Licensing*.

Kalamazoo, MI: W.E. Upjohn Institute Press. Forthcoming.

Kleiner, Morris M. (2015). "Reforming Occupational Licensing Policies." *The Hamilton Project*. Brookings Institution. http:// www. hamiltonproject.org/papers/reforming_occupational_licensing_policies/.

Kleiner, Robert S. Gay. & Karen, Greene. (1982). "Barriers to Labor Migration: The Case of Occupational Licensing." *Industrial Relations*, *21*, no. 3, 383-391.

Kleiner, Morris M. & Alan, Krueger B. (2010). "The Prevalence and Effects of Occupational Licensing." *British Journal of Industrial Relations*, *48*, no. 4, 676-687.

Kleiner, Morris M. & Alan, Krueger B. (2013). "Analyzing the Extent and Influence of Occupational Licensing on the Labor Market." *Journal of Labor Economics*, *31*, no. 2, S173-S202.

Kleiner, Morris M., Allison, Marier., Kyoung, Won Park. & Coady, Wing. (2014). "Relaxing Occupational Licensing Requirements: Analyzing Wages and Prices for a Medical Service." NBER Working Paper 19906.

Kleiner, Morris M. & Kyoung, Won Park. (2010). "Battles Among Licensed Occupations: Analyzing Government Regulations on Labor Market Outcomes for Dentists and Hygienists." NBER Working Paper 16560.

Kleiner, Morris M. & Kyong, Won Park. (2014). "Life, Limbs and Licensing: Occupational Regulation, Wages, and Workplace Safety of Electricians, 1992-2007." *Monthly Labor Review.*, U.S. Bureau of Labor Statistics.

Kleiner, Morris M. & Richard M. Todd. (2009). "Mortgage Broker Regulations that Matter: Analyzing Earnings, Employment, and Outcomes for Consumers." *Studies of Labor Market Intermediation.*

Kleiner, Morris M. & Robert, Kudrle T. (2000). "Does Regulation Affect Economic Outcomes? The Case of Dentistry." *Journal of Law and Economics, 43*, no. 2: 547-582. The University of Chicago Press.

Knapp, Sarah. (2013). "Can LegalZoom Be the Answer to the Justice Gap?" *Georgetown Journal of Legal Ethics, 26*, no. 4: 821-836.

Kuo, Yong-Fang., Figaro, Loresto L., Jr. Linda, Rounds R. & James, Goodwin S. ( 2013). "States with the Least Restrictive Regulations Experienced the Largest Increase in Patients Seen By Nurse Practitioners." *Health Affairs, 32*, no. 7, 1236-1243.

Larsen, Bradley. (2015). "Occupational Licensing and Quality: Distributional and Heterogeneous Effects in the Teaching Profession." Working paper. http://web.stanford.edu/~bjlarsen/Larsen%20(2015)%20Occupational%20 licensing%20 and%20quality.pdf.

Law, Marc T. & Sukkoo, Kim. (2005). "Specialization and Regulation: The Rise of Professionals and the Emergence of Occupational Licensing Regulation." *Journal of Economic History, 65*, no. 3, 723-756. Cambridge University Press.

Legal Services Corporation. (2009). *Documenting the Justice Gap in America: The Current Unmet Civil Legal Needs of Low-Income Americans.*http://www.lsc.gov/sites/default/files/LSC/pdfs/documenting_the_justice_gap_in_ame rica_2009.pdf.

Lenz, Elizabeth R., Mary, O'Neil., Mundinger, Robert L., Kane Sarah C. Hopkins. & Susan X. Lin. (2004). "Primary Care Outcomes in Patients Treated by Nurse Practitioners or Physicians: Two-Year Follow-Up." *Medical Care Research and Review, 61*, no. 3, 332-51.

Liang, J. N. & Jonathan, D. Ogur. (1987). "Restrictions on Dental Auxiliaries: An Economic Policy Analysis." Bureau of Economics. Washington, DC: Federal Trade Commission.

Lopez, Fanny., Nancy, Younan. & Rebecca, Tancredi. (2014). "Foreign-Educated Engineers: Barriers to Employment and Professional Relicensing in Illinois." Illinois Coalition for Immigrant and Refugee Rights.http://icirr.org/content/report-discusses-barriers-immigrant-engineers-illinois.

Loten, Angus. & Needleman, Sarah E. (2014). "State Licensing Boards Under Fire from Within." *The Wall Street Journal*. http:// www.wsj.com/ articles/state-licensing-boards-under-fire- from-within-1409184515.

Luca, Michael. (2011). "Reviews, Reputation, and Revenue: The Case of Yelp.com." HBS Working Paper 12-016. http:// dx.doi.org/ 10.2139/ ssrn.1928601.

Maine Department of Professional and Financial Regulation. (2015). Private Correspondence. Maine Revised Statutes Title 32 § 60-J. http:// legislature.maine.gov/statutes/32/title32sec60-J.html.

Massachusetts Department of Health and Human Services. *Good Moral Character Requirements for Licensing*. http:// www.mass.gov/ eohhs/ gov/ departments/dph/programs/hcq/dhpl/nursing/licensing/good-moral-character-requirements-for-licensure.html.

Massachusetts General Hospital Imaging. (2011). "Imaging News." http:// www.massgeneral.org/imaging/news/newsarticle.aspx?id=2807.

Meyer, Peter B. & Osborne, Anastasiya M. (2005). "Proposed category system for 1960-2000 Census Occupations." U.S. Bureau of Labor Statistics. Working Paper 383.

Michigan PublicAct 267. (2014). http:// www.legislature.mi.gov/ documents/ 2013-2014/publicact/pdf/2014-PA-0267.pdf.

Michigan Department of Licensing and Regulatory Affairs. (2012). *Office of Regulatory Reinvention Issues Recommendations to Deregulate 18 Occupations; Eliminate 9 Boards*. http:// www.michigan.gov/ lara/ 0, 4601,7-154-10573_11472-275935--RSS,00.html.

Michigan Licensing and Regulatory Affairs. (2015). Private correspondence.

Military Officers Association of America. (2015). "Military Spouse Licensure: Is Your State on Board?"http:// moaablogs.org/ spouse/ 2012/ 12/military-spouse-licensure-is-your-state-on- board/.

Minnesota Senate Bill 784. (2015). http:// www.senate.leg.state.mn.us/ bills/ billinf.php?ls=89&billnum=784.

Minton, Todd D. (2013). "Jail Inmates at Midyear 2012 – Statistical Tables." U.S. Department of Justice, Bureau of Justice Statistics. http://www.bjs.gov/content/pub/pdf/jim12st.pdf.

Molloy, Raven., Smith, Christopher L. & Abigail, Wozniak. (2011). "Internal Migration in the United States." *Journal of Economic Perspectives*, *25*, no. 3, 173-196. American Economic Association.

Molloy, Raven., Smith, Christopher L. & Abigail, Wozniak. (2014). "Declining Migration within the U.S.: The Role of the Labor Market." NBER Working Paper 20065.

Montana Legislature. (2015). House Bill 363. http:// leg.mt.gov/ bills/ 2015/ billhtml/HB0363.htm.

Moore, Michael G. & Greg, Kearsley. (2012). "Distance Education: A Systems View of Online Learning." Third edition. Wadsworth Cengage Learning.http://www.cengagebrain.com.au/content/moore20992_1111520992_02.01_chapter01.pdf.

National Center for Education Statistics. (2013). *2011-12 National Postsecondary Student Aid Study*. U.S. Department of Education. http://nces.ed.gov/pubs2013/2013165.pdf.

National Consumer Law Center. (2014). *State Laws and Statutes That Suspend Professional Licenses and Certificates*. http://www.jwj.org/wp-content/uploads/2015/02/State-Laws-and-Statutes-That-Suspend-Professional-Licenses-and-Certificates.pdf.

National Council for State Authorization Reciprocity Agreements. http://nc-sara.org/.

National Council of State Boards of Nursing. (2015). "25 Nurse Licensure Compact (NLC) States." https:// www.ncsbn.org/ NLC_ Implementation_ 2015.pdf.

National Economic Council and Council of Economic Advisers. (2013). *The Fast Track to Civilian Employment: Streamlining Credentialing and Licensing for Service Members, Veterans, and their Spouses.* https://www.whitehouse.gov/sites/default/files/docs/military_credentialing_and_licens ing_report_2-24-2013_final.pdf.

National Employment Law Project. Interview by National Economic Council. 2015. Washington, DC.

Naylor, Mary D. & Ellen T. Kurtzman. (2010). "The Role of Nurse Practitioners in Reinventing Primary Care." *Health Affairs*, *29*, no. 5: 893-899.

Neighly, Madeline., Maurice, Emsellem. & Anastasia, Christman. (2014). "A Healthy Balance: Expanding Expanding Health Care Job Opportunities for Californians with a Criminal Record While Ensuring Patient Safety and Security. " National Employment Law Project. http:// www.nelp.org/ content/uploads/2015/01/Healthy-Balance-Full-Report.pdf.

Newhouse, Robin P. et al. (2011). "Advanced Practice Nurse Outcomes 1990-2008: A Systematic Review." *Nursing Economics*, *29*, no. 5: 230-250. https://www.nursingeconomics.net/ce/2013/article3001021.pdf.

North Carolina State Board of Dental Examiners v. Federal Trade Commission, 135 S. Ct. 1101. (2015). http:// www.supremecourt.gov/ opinions/14pdf/13-534_19m2.pdf.

North Carolina General Assembly Legislative Services Office. (2014). "Occupational Licensing Agencies Should Not be Centralized, but Stronger Oversight is Needed." *Final Report to the Joint Legislative Program Evaluation Oversight Committee* no. 2014-15. http:// www. ncleg.net/PED/Reports/documents/OccLic/OccLic_Report.pdf.

Nosko, Chris and Steven Tadelis. (2015). "The Limits of Reputation in Platform Markets: An Empirical Analysis and Field Experiment." NBER Working Paper 20830.

NursingLicensure.org. (2015). *LPN/LVN and Registered Nurse License Requirements by State.*http://www.nursinglicensure.org/.

Olson, Mancur. 1965. "The Logic of Collective Action: Public Goods and the Theory of Groups."

Harvard University Press. Parker v. Brown, 317 U.S. 341. 1943.

Paul, Chris. (1984). "Physician Licensure Legislation and the Quality of Medical Care." *Atlantic Economic Journal*, *12*, no. 4, 18-30.

Pashigian, B. Peter. (1979). "Occupational Licensing and the Interstate Mobility of Professionals." *Journal of Law and Economics*, *22*, no. 1: 1-25.

Persico, Nicola. (2015). "The Political Economy of Occupational Licensing Associations." *Journal of Law, Economics, & Organization*, *31*, no. 2: 213-241. Oxford Journals.

Peterson, Brenton D., Pandya, Sonal S. & David, Leblang. (2014). "Doctors With Borders: Occupational Licensing as an Implicit Barrier to High Skill Migration." *Public Choice*, *160*, no. 1-2, 45-63.

Pew Health Professions Committee. (1995). "Reforming Health Care Workforce Regulation: Policy Considerations for the 21st Century." *Report of the Taskforce on Health Care Workforce Regulation.* http://www.futurehealth.ucsf.edu/Content/29/199512_Reforming_Health_Care_Workforce_Regulation_Policy_Considerations_for_the_21st_Century.pdf.

Powell, Benjamin. & Evgeny, Vorotnikov. (2012). "Real Estate Continuing Education: Rent Seeking or Improvement in Service Quality?" *Eastern Economic Journal*, *38*, no. 1, 57-73.

Phelan, John J. (1974). "Economic Report [on the] Regulation of the Television Repair Industry in Louisiana and California: A Case Study: Staff Report to the Federal Trade Commission." 23. U.S. Government Printing Office.

Rhode, Deborah. (1981). "Policing the Professional Monopoly: A Constitutional and Empirical Analysis of Unauthorized Practice Prohibitions." *Stanford Law Review*, *34*, no. 1, 1-112.

Rodriguez, Michelle Natividad. & Maurice, Emsellem. (2011). "65 Million 'Need Not Apply': The Case for Reforming Criminal Background Checks for Employment." National Employment Law Center. http:// www. nelp. org/content/uploads/2015/03/65_Million_Need_Not_Apply.pdf.

Saks, Raven E. & Abigail, Wozniak. (2011). "Labor Reallocation over the Business Cycle: New Evidence from Internal Migration." *Journal of Labor Economics*, *29*, no. 4, 697-739. The University of Chicago Press.

Shapiro, Carl. (1986). "Investment, Moral Hazard, and Occupational Licensing." *Review of Economic Studies*, *53*, no. 5, 843-862.

Shepard, Lawrence. (1978). "Licensing Restrictions and the Cost of Dental Care." *Journal of Law and Economics*, *21*, no. 1, 187–201. The University of Chicago Press.

Shimberg, Benjamin. (1980). *Occupational Licensing: A Public Perspective.* Educational Testing Service.

Shimberg, Benjamin. & Doug, Roederer. (1994). "Questions a Legislator Should Ask." Second Edition. Lexington, KY: The Council on Licensure, Enforcement and Regulation.

Slivinski, Stephen. (2015). "Bootstraps Tangles in Red Tape: How Occupational Licensing Hinders Low-Income Entrepreneurship." Goldwater Institute with support from the Ewing Marion Kauffman Foundation. https:// goldwater- media.s3. amazonaws.com/ cms_ page_ media/2015/4/15/OccLicensingKauffman.pdf.

Smith, Adam. (1776). *An Inquiry into the Nature and Causes of the Wealth of Nations*, Book I, Ch. 10, Part II.

Spetz, Joanne. (2013). "Scope-of-Practice Laws for Nurse Practitioners Limit Cost Savings that Can Be Achieved in Retail Clinics." *Health Affairs*, *32*, no. 11, 1977-1984.

St George, Ian., et al. (2009). "How Safe is Telenursing from Home?" *Collegian*, *16*, no. 3, 119-123.

Stange, Kevin. (2014). "How Does Provider Supply and Regulation Influence Health Care Markets? Evidence from Nurse Practitioners and Physician Assistants." *Journal of Health Economics*, *33*, 1-27.

Stanik-Hutt, Julie., et al. (2013). "The Quality and Effectiveness of Care Provided by Nurse Practitioners." *Journal for Nurse Practitioners*, *9*, no. 8, 492-500.

Starr, Paul. (1982). *The Social Transformation of American Medicine*. New York, NY: Basic Books.

Starr, Paul. (2009). "Professionalization and Public Health: Historical Legacies, Continuing Dilemmas." *Journal of Public Health Management Practice, 15*, no. 6, S26-S30.

Stigler, George. (1971). "The Theory of Economic Regulation." *The Bell Journal of Economics and Management Science, 2*, no. 1, 3-21.

Swankin, David A. (2012). "Regulation of the Professions: Where Have We Been? Where Are We Going?" *FARB Speech.*

Swankin, David A., Rebecca, LeBuhn. & Artem, Gulish. (2010). "Discussion Draft: Building a Better Mousetrap to Address Scope of Practice Issues." *Citizen Advocacy Center.*

Task Force to Expand Access to Civil Legal Services in New York. (2010). *Report to the Chief Judge of the State of New York.* https:// www.nycourts.gov/ip/access-civil-legal-services/PDF/CLS-TaskForceReport.pdf.

Texas Department of Licensing and Regulation. "Guidelines for License Applicants with Criminal Convictions." http:// www.tdlr.texas.gov/crimconvict.htm.

Texas Legislature. (2015). Senate Bill 202.

Texas Occupations Code, Title 2, Chapter 53, Subchapter B, Sec. 53.025. http://www.statutes.legis.state.tx.us/Docs/OC/htm/OC.53.htm.

The Legal Action Center. *After Prison: Roadblocks to Reentry: A Report on State Legal Barriers FacingPeople with Criminal Records.* http:// www.lac.org/roadblocks-to- reentry/main.php?view=law&subaction=4.

Thierer, Adam., Christopher, Koopman., Anne, Hobson. & Chris, Kuiper. (2015). "How the Internet, the Sharing Economy, and Reputational Feedback Mechanisms Solve the 'Lemons Problem.'" Mercatus Working Paper. http:// mercatus.org/ sites/ default/ files/ Thierer- Lemons-Problem.pdf.

Thornton, Robert J. & Timmons, Edward J. (2010). "The Licensing of Barbers in the USA." *British Journal of Industrial Relations, 48*, no. 4, 740-757.

Thornton, Robert J. & Timmons, Edward J. (2013). "Licensing One of the World's Oldest Professions: Massage." *Journal of Law and Economics, 56*, no. 2, 371-388. The University of Chicago Press.

Thornton, Robert J. & Timmons, Edward J. ( 2015). "The De-Licensing of Occupations in the United States." *Monthly Labor Review.* U.S. Bureau of Labor Statistics.

U.S. Department of Health and Human Services. (2009). *Pandemic and All-Hazards Preparedness Act, Telehealth Report to Congress.* http:// www.phe.gov/Preparedness/legal/pahpa/Documents/telehealthrtc-091207.pdf.

U.S. Department of Labor. License Finder. http:// www.careeronestop.org/toolkit/training/find-licenses.aspx.

U.S. Department of the Treasury and U.S. Department of Defense. (2012). *Supporting our Military Families: Best Practices for Streamlining Occupational Licensing Across State Lines.* http:// www.defense.gov/home/pdf/Occupational_Licensing_and_Military_Spouses_Report_vFINAL.PDF.

Vallas, Rebecca. & Sharon, Dietrich. (2014). "One Strike and You're Out: How We Can Eliminate Barriers to Economic Security and Mobility for People with Criminal Records." Center for American Progress. https://www.americanprogress.org/issues/poverty/report/2014/12/02/102308/one-strike-and-youre-out/.

Washington State Bar Association. (2015). "Limited License Legal Technicians (LLLT)." http:// www.wsba.org/ licensing-and-lawyer-conduct/limited-licenses/legal-technicians.

Wheelan, Charles. (1999). "Politics or Public Interest? An Empirical Examination of Occupational Licensure." The University of Chicago, unpublished manuscript.

White, William D. (1980). "Mandatory Licensing of Registered Nurses: Introduction and Impact." *Occupational Licensure and Regulation.* Washington, DC: American Enterprise Institute Press.

Whitney, Eric. (2015). "States Review Laws Revoking Licenses for Student Loan Defaults." *NPR.* http://www.npr.org/2015/04/08/398037156/States-review-laws-revoking-licenses-for- student-loan-defaults.

Wozniak, Abigail. (2010). "Are College Graduates More Responsive to Distant Labor Market Opportunities?" *Journal of Human Resources, 45*(4), 944-970.

## End Notes

[1] Council of Economic Advisers. 2015. *The Economic Report of the President.*

[2] Executive Order 13563. January 18, 2011. Federal Register 76(14).

[3] Kleiner, Morris M. and Alan B. Krueger. 2013. "Analyzing the Extent and Influence of Occupational Licensing on the Labor Market." *Journal of Labor Economics* 31, no. 2: S173-S202.

[4] Carpenter, Dick, Angela C. Erickson, Lisa Knepper, and John K. Ross. 2012. "License to Work: A National Study of Burdens from Occupational Licensing." Institute for Justice. https://www.ij.org/licensetowork.

[5] Brinegar, Pamela L. and Kara L. Schmitt. 1992. "State Occupational and Professional Licensure." *The Book of the States* 567–80. Lexington, KY: Council of State Governments.

[6] There are a number of terms used throughout this report. A *license* represents formal permission from a government body to practice in an occupation. Licensing laws not only determine whether an individual can practice, but they also often enumerate what services she can provide as part of her practice. This is commonly referred to as *scope of practice*. In addition to occupational licensing, there are two other less restrictive forms of traditional occupational regulation: state certification and registration. *State certification*, or "right-to-title," means that individuals seeking to assume a profession's official title must obtain the permission of the government, but anyone is allowed to perform the duties of the profession, regardless of whether or not they have been certified. Certification can also be done by private certifying bodies, which give their imprimatur to workers who have met their standards. *Registration* is the least restrictive form of occupational regulation. It generally just involves individuals paying a fee and filing their names, addresses, and qualifications with the government. This ensures that practitioners can be reached in the event of a complaint, thereby supporting civil remedies for consumer harm. Benjamin Shimberg. 1980. *Occupational Licensing: A Public Perspective*. Educational Testing Service.

[7] Kleiner, Morris M. 2015. "Reforming Occupational Licensing Policies." *The Hamilton Project.* Brookings Institution. http:// www.hamiltonproject.org/ papers/ reforming_ occupational_ licensing_policies/.

[8] Kleiner (2015).

[9] Vallas, Rebecca and Sharon Dietrich. 2014. "One Strike and You're Out: How We Can Eliminate Barriers to Economic Security and Mobility for People with Criminal Records." Center for American Progress. https:// www.americanprogress.org/ issues/ poverty/ report/ 2014/ 12/ 02/102308/one-strike-and-youre-out/.

[10] While this report uses various specific professions as examples to illustrate broader trends in licensing, it is beyond the scope of this report to recommend reforms to State or other regulations for specific occupations.

[11] Barnes, Linda L. 2003. "The Acupuncture Wars: The Professionalizing of American Acupuncture—A View from Massachusetts." *Medical Anthropology* 22, no. 3: 261-301.

[12] Akerlof, George A. 1970. "The Market for Lemons: Quality Uncertainty and the Market Mechanism." *Quarterly Journal of Economics* 84, no. 3: 488-500; Kleiner, Morris M. 2000. "Occupational Licensing." *Journal of Economic Perspectives* 14, no. 4: 189-202. American Economic Association; Shapiro, Carl. 1986. "Investment, Moral Hazard, and Occupational Licensing." *Review of Economic Studies* 53, no. 5: 843-862.

[13] Smith, Adam. 1776. *An Inquiry into the Nature and Causes of the Wealth of Nations*, Book I, Ch. 10, Part II; Kleiner, Morris M. 2006. "Licensing Occupations: Ensuring Quality or Restriction Competition?" *W.E. Upjohn Institute for Employment Research* 1-15. Kalamazoo, MI: Upjohn Institute Press; Friedman, Milton and Simon Kuznets. 1954. "Income from Independent Professional Practice." New York, NY: NBER; Law, Marc T., and Sukkoo Kim. 2005. "Specialization and Regulation: The Rise of Professionals and the Emergence of Occupational Licensing Regulation." *Journal of Economic History* 65, no. 3: 723-756. Cambridge University Press.

[14] Kleiner and Krueger (2013), Westat Data; UST calculations.

[15] Kleiner and Krueger (2013), Westat Data; UST and CEA calculations.

[16] Slivinski, Stephen. 2015. "Bootstraps Tangles in Red Tape: How Occupational Licensing Hinders Low-Income Entrepreneurship." Goldwater Institute with support from the Ewing

Marion Kauffman Foundation. https://goldwater-media.s3.amazonaws.com/ cms_page_media/2015/4/15/OccLicensingKauffman.pdf.

[17] Kleiner and Krueger (2013), Westat Data; UST and CEA calculations.

[18] Slivinski (2015) finds that low-income entrepreneurship activity is substantially reduced in States that license a large fraction of low-income occupations.

[19] U.S. Department of the Treasury and U.S. Department of Defense (2012).

[20] Shimberg (1980); Swankin, David A. 2012. "Regulation of the Professions: Where Have We Been? Where Are We Going?" *FARB Speech.*

[21] Kleiner, Morris M., Allison Marier, Kyoung Won Park, and Coady Wing. 2014. "Relaxing Occupational Licensing Requirements: Analyzing Wages and Prices for a Medical Service." NBER Working Paper 19906.

[22] Liang, J. N. and Jonathan D. Ogur. 1987. "Restrictions on Dental Auxiliaries: An Economic Policy Analysis." Bureau of Economics. Washington, DC: Federal Trade Commission.

[23] Federman, Maya N., David E. Harrington, and Kathy J. Krynski. 2006. "The Impact of State Licensing Regulations on Low-Skilled Immigrants: The Case of Vietnamese Manicurists." *American Economic Review* 96, no. 2: 237-241.

[24] Kleiner, Morris M. and Kyoung Won Park. 2010. "Battles Among Licensed Occupations: Analyzing Government Regulations on Labor Market Outcomes for Dentists and Hygienists." NBER Working Paper 16560.

[25] Kleiner and Krueger (2013), Westat Data; UST calculations.

[26] Kleiner, Morris M. and Alan B. Krueger. 2010. "The Prevalence and Effects of Occupational Licensing." *British Journal of Industrial Relations* 48, no. 4: 676-687.

[27] Gittleman, Maury, Mark A. Klee, and Morris M. Kleiner. 2015. "Analyzing the Labor Market Outcomes of Occupational Licensing." NBER Working Paper 20961; Gittleman, Maury and Morris M. Kleiner. 2013. "Wage Effects of Unionization and Occupational Licensing Coverage in the United States." NBER Working Paper 19061; Klee, Mark A. 2013. "How Do Professional Licensing Regulations Affect Practitioners? New Evidence." U.S. Bureau of Labor Statistics, SEHSD Working Paper 2013-30.

[28] Wozniak, Abigail. 2010. "Are College Graduates More Responsive to Distant Labor Market Opportunities?" *Journal of Human Resources* 45, no. 4: 944-970; Blanchard, Olivier and Lawrence Katz. 1992. "Regional Evolutions." *Brookings Papers on Economic Activity* no. 1: 1-75.

[29] Gay, Robert, Karen Greene, and Morris Kleiner. 1982. "Barriers to Labor Migration: The Case of Occupational Licensing." *Industrial Relations* 21, no. 3: 383-391; Holen (1965) also finds that dentists and lawyers are less mobile than physicians, for whom she asserts State licensure restrictions represent less of a barrier to moving across States. Holen, Arlene. 1965. "Effects of Professional Licensing Arrangements on Interstate Labor Mobility and Resource Allocation." *Journal of Political Economy* 73, no. 5: 492-498.

[30] Johnson, Janna E. and Morris M. Kleiner. 2015. "Is Occupational Licensing a Barrier to Interstate Migration?" Forthcoming.

[31] Kleiner and Krueger (2013). The data from the 1950s come from the Council of State Governments, the data for the 1960s are from Greene (1969), the data for the 1980s are from Kleiner (1990), and the data for 2000 are from Kleiner (2006); Greene, Karen. 1969. "Occupational Licensing and the Supply of Nonprofessional Manpower." Washington, DC: Manpower Administration, U.S. Department of Labor; Kleiner, Morris M. 1990. "Are There Economic Rents for More Restrictive Occupational Licensing Practices?' *42nd Annual Proceedings. United States: Industrial Relations Research Association* 177-185.

[32] Kleiner and Krueger (2013).

[33] Gittleman, Klee, and Kleiner (2015).

[34] Gittleman, Klee, and Kleiner (2015) note that sample attrition likely biases their estimates upward, but the relatively low percentage of workers in some universally licensed

occupations (such as surgeons) who report having a license or certification suggests that SIPP-derived estimates of licensing prevalence may be biased downward.

[35] Kleiner and Krueger (2013), Westat data; CEA calculations.

[36] To make the adjustment, we use Kleiner and Krueger's estimates of the shares of State-licensed workers in each occupation in 2008, and adjust for changes in occupational mix back to 1968, taking advantage of a h istorically consistent occupational classification system contained in the Integrated Public Use Microdata Series version of the Current Population Survey. Note that the aggregate share licensed according to the Kleiner and Krueger estimate does not match the counterfactual percent licensed in 2008 because the proportion of workers within each occupation is different in the Kleiner and Krueger data and in the Current Population Survey. Meyer, Peter B. and Anastasiya M. Osborne. 2005. "Proposed category system for 1960-2000 Census Occupations." U.S. Bureau of Labor Statistics. Working Paper 383; Alexander, J. Trent, Sarah Flood, Katie Genadek, Miriam King, Steven Ruggles, Matthew B. Schroeder, and Brandon Trample. 2010. Integrated Public Use Microdata Series, Current Population Survey: Version 3.0. [Machine-readable database]

[37] Cairo, Isabel. 2013. "The Slowdown in Business Employment Dynamics: The Role of Changing Skill Demands." Job Market Paper. http:// www.econ.upf.edu/ gpefm/ jm/ pdf/ paper/JMP%20Cairo.pdf.

[38] Starr, Paul. 2009. "Professionalization and Public Health: Historical Legacies, Continuing Dilemmas." *Journal of Public Health Management Practice* 15, no. 6: S26-S30.

[39] Starr, Paul. 1982. *The Social Transformation of American Medicine*. New York, NY: Basic Books; Law and Kim (2005) find evidence from the Progressive Era that licensing was adopted in response to increased specialization and technological developments that made it more difficult for consumers to judge the quality of professional services.

[40] Arrow, Kenneth J. 1971. "Essays in the Theory of Risk-Bearing." Chicago, IL: Markham Publishing Co.; Arrow, Kenneth J. 1963. "Uncertainty and the Welfare Economics of Medical Care. 1963." *American Economic Review* 53, no. 5: 941–969; Kleiner (2006).

[41] Law and Kim (2005).

[42] Friedman, Milton. 1962. "Capitalism and Freedom." Chicago, IL: The University of Chicago Press; Olson, Mancur. 1965. "The Logic of Collective Action: Public Goods and the Theory of Groups." Harvard University Press; Stigler, George. 1971. "The Theory of Economic Regulation." *The Bell Journal of Economics and Management Science* 2, no. 1: 3-21.

[43] Wheelan, Charles. 1999. "Politics or Public Interest? An Empirical Examination of Occupational Licensure." The University of Chicago, unpublished manuscript; White, William D. 1980. "Mandatory Licensing of Registered Nurses: Introduction and Impact." *Occupational Licensure and Regulation.* Washington, DC: American Enterprise Institute Press; Paul, Chris. 1984. "Physician Licensure Legislation and the Quality of Medical Care." *Atlantic Economic Journal* 12, no. 4: 18-30.

[44] Thornton, Robert J. and Edward J. Timmons. 2015. "The De-Licensing of Occupations in the United States." *Monthly Labor Review.* U.S. Bureau of Labor Statistics.

[45] Swankin (2012).

[46] Kleiner (2015).

[47] Carpenter et al. (2012).

[48] Carpenter et al. (2012).

[49] Neighly, Madeline, Maurice Emsellem, and Anastasia Christman. 2014. "A Healthy Balance: Expanding Expanding Health Care Job Opportunities for Californians with a Criminal Record While Ensuring Patient Safety and Security." National Employment Law Project. http://www.nelp.org/content/uploads/2015/01/Healthy-Balance-Full- Report.pdf.

[50] Davis, Steven J. and John Haltiwanger. 2014. "Labor Market Fluidity and Economic Performance." NBER Working Paper 20479.

[51] American Community Survey 2001-2013; CEA calculations. 3.4 percent of the workforce reported working from home at least once a week in 2001 versus 4.4 percent in 2013.

[52] MassachusettsGeneralHospitalImaging.2011. "Imaging News." http:// www. massgeneral.org/imaging/news/newsarticle.aspx?id=2807.

[53] St George, Ian, et al. 2009. "How Safe is Telenursing from Home?" *Collegian* 16, no. 3: 119-123.

[54] U.S. Department of Health and Human Services. 2009. *Pandemic and All-Hazards Preparedness Act, Telehealth Report to Congress.* http:// www.phe.gov/ Preparedness/ legal/pahpa/Documents/telehealthrtc-091207.pdf.

[55] National Council of State Boards of Nursing. 2015. "25 Nurse Licensure Compact (NLC) States." https:// www.ncsbn.org/ NLC_Implementation_2015.pdf; American Nurses Association. 2013. "Nurse Licensure Compact." http:// www.nursingworld.org/ MainMenuCategories/Policy-Advocacy/State/Legislative-Agenda-Reports/LicensureCompact/INLC-TalkingPoints.pdf.

[56] Hadfield, Gillian K. 2014. "The Cost of Law: Promoting Access to Justice through the (Un)Corporate Practice of Law." *International Review of Law and Economics* 38: 43-63; Knapp, Sarah. 2013. "Can LegalZoom Be the Answer to the Justice Gap?" *Georgetown Journal of Legal Ethics* 26, no. 4: 821-836.

[57] For example, Kleiner et al. (2014) find that more restrictive scope of practice licensing for nurse practitioners increases physician wages and hours worked, and decreases NP wages and hours worked.

[58] Swankin, David A., Rebecca LeBuhn, and Artem Gulish. 2010. "Discussion Draft: Building a Better Mousetrap to Address Scope of Practice Issues." *Citizen Advocacy Center*.

[59] Kleiner, Morris M. *Guild-Ridden Labor Markets: The Curious Case of Occupational Licensing*. Kalamazoo, MI: W.E. Upjohn Institute Press. Forthcoming.

[60] Legal Services Corporation. 2009. *Documenting the Justice Gap in America: The Current Unmet Civil Legal Needs of Low-Income Americans.* http:// www.lsc.gov/ sites/ default/ files/LSC/pdfs/documenting_the_justice_gap_in_america_2009.pdf.

[61] Judicial Council of California. 2004. *Statewide Action Plan for Serving Self-Represented Litigants*. http:// www.courts.ca.gov/documents/selfreplitsrept.pdf.

[62] Task Force to Expand Access to Civil Legal Services in New York. 2010. *Report to the Chief Judge of the State of New York.* https://www.nycourts.gov/ip/access-civil-legal-services/PDF/CLS-TaskForce REPORT.pdf.

[63] Klein, Linda. 2010. *Report on the Survey of Judges on the Impact of the Economic Downturn on Representation in the Courts.* ABA Coalition for Justice.http:// www. americanbar.org/content/dam/aba/migrated/JusticeCenter/PublicDocuments/CoalitionforJusticeSurv eyReport.authcheckdam.pdf.

[64] Ambrogi, Robert. 2015. "Who Says you Need a Law Degree to Practice Law?" *Washington Post.* http:// www.washingtonpost.com/ opinions/ closing-the-justice gap/2015/03/13/a5f576c8-c754-11e4-aa1a-86135599fb0f_story.html.

[65] Washington State Bar Association. 2015. "Limited License Legal Technicians (LLLT)." http:// www.wsba.org/ licensing-and-lawyer-conduct/limited-licenses/legal-technicians.

[66] Institute of Medicine of the National Academies. 2010. "The Future of Nursing: Focus on Scope of Practice." http://www.iom.edu/Reports/2010/The-Future-of-Nursing-Leading-Change-Advancing-Health/Report-Brief-Scope- of-Practice.aspx. APRNs have completed specialty-specific graduate programs and fall into four main categories: nurse anesthetists, nurse midwives, clinical nurse specialists, and nurse practitioners. The term Advanced Practice Nurse (APN) is also sometimes used interchangeably, but that term can also be used more broadly and has no single generally accepted regulatory definition; Newhouse, Robin P., et al. 2011. "Advanced Practice Nurse Outcomes 1990-2008: A Systematic Review." *Nursing Economics* 29, no. 5: 230-250; American Association of Nurse Practitioners. 2015. "2015 Nurse Practitioner State Practice Environment." http:// www.aanp.org/ images/

documents/State-leg-reg/stateregulatorymap.pdf; Iglehart, John K. "Expanding the Role of Advanced Nurse Practitioners—Risks and Rewards." Th*e New England Journal of Medicine* 368, no. 20: 1935-1941.

[67] Stanik-Hutt, Julie, et al. 2013. "The Quality and Effectiveness of Care Provided by Nurse Practitioners." *Journal for Nurse Practitioners* 9, no. 8: 492-500; Institute of Medicine (2010); Lenz, Elizabeth R., Mary O'Neil Mundinger, Robert L. Kane, Sarah C. Hopkins, and Susan X. Lin. 2004. "Primary Care Outcomes in Patients Treated by Nurse Practitioners or Physicians: Two-Year Follow-Up." *Medical Care Research and Review* 61, no. 3: 332-51.

[68] Kuo, Yong-Fang, Figaro L. Loresto Jr., Linda R. Rounds, and James S. Goodwin. 2013. "States with the Least Restrictive Regulations Experienced the Largest Increase in Patients Seen By Nurse Practitioners." *Health Affairs* 32, no. 7: 1236-1243.

[69] Stange, Kevin. 2014. "How Does Provider Supply and Regulation Influence Health Care Markets? Evidence from Nurse Practitioners and Physician Assistants." *Journal of Health Economics* 33: 1-27.

[70] Institute of Education Sciences. 2015. *The Condition of Education 2015*. U.S. Department of Education. http://nces.ed.gov/pubs2015/2015144.pdf.

[71] Allen, Elaine and Jeff Seaman. 2014. "Grade Change: Tracking Online Education in the United States." *Babson Survey Research Group*. http:// www.onlinelearningsurvey. com/ reports/gradechange.pdf.

[72] National Center for Education Statistics. 2013. *2011-12 National Postsecondary Student Aid Study*. U.S. Department of Education. http:// nces.ed.gov/ pubs2013/ 2013165.pdf. Tabulated from PowerStats; CEA calculations.

[73] Moore, Michael G. and Greg Kearsley. 2012. "Distance Education: A Systems View of Online Learning." Third edition. Wadswort Cengage Learning. http:// www. cengagebrain.com.au/content/moore20992_1111520992_02.01_chapter01.pdf.

[74] See nursinglicensure.org for a full list of State board requirements. NursingLicensure.org. 2015. *LPN/LVN and Registered Nurse License Requirements by State*. http:// www. nursinglicensure.org/.

[75] Cowen, Tyler and Alex Tabarrok. 2015. "The End of Asymmetric Information." *Cato Unbound*. http:// www.cato- unbound.org/ 2015/ 04/ 06/ alex-tabarrok-tyler-cowen/end-asymmetric-information; Thierer, Adam, Christopher Koopman, Anne Hobson, and Chris Kuiper. 2015. "How the Internet, the Sharing Economy, and Reputationa l Feedback Mechanisms Solve the 'Lemons Problem.'" Mercatus Working Paper. http:// mercatus.org/sites/default/files/Thierer-Lemons-Problem.pdf.

[76] Brown, Jennifer and John Morgan. 2006. "Reputation in Online Auctions: The Market for Trust." *California Management Review* 49, no. 1: 61-81.

[77] Luca, Michael. 2011. "Reviews, Reputation, and Revenue: The Case of Yelp.com." *HBS Working Paper*.

[78] American Bar Association National Inventory of Collateral Consequences of Conviction. http:// www.abacollateralconsequences.org/search/.

[79] Alabama Administrative Code r. 330-X-3-.01; California Business and Professions Code § 3057. http:// optometry.ca.gov/formspubs/endorsement.pdf.

[80] This estimate includes individuals who have State records of arrests or subsequent dispositions. Most convictions are for misdemeanors and non-serious infractions, and many records are for arrests without convictions. As evident from the range in estimates cited above, there is considerable uncertainty surrounding the total number of Americans with criminal records. The Department of Justice reports that over 100.5 million Americans have state criminal history records. However, individuals may have records in multiple States, so the National Employment Law Center suggests discounting the DOJ's estimate by 30 percent, resulting in an estimate of closer to one in four adult Americans with a criminal record. On the other hand, in some states, misdemeanor arrests for less serious crimes do not require

fingerprinting, and thus the DOJ's estimate may undercount these individuals. Bureau of Justice Statistics. 2012. "Survey of State Criminal History Information Systems, 2012." U.S. Department of Justice. https://www.ncjrs.gov/pdffiles1/bjs/grants/244563.pdf; Vallas and Dietrich (2014); Rodriguez, Michelle Natividad and Maurice Emsellem. 2011. "65 Million 'Need Not Apply': The Case for Reforming Criminal Background Checks for Employment." National Employment Law Center. http:// www.nelp.org/ content/ uploads/ 2015/03/65_Million_Need_Not_Apply.pdf.

81 Carson, E. Ann and William J. Sabol. 2012. "Prisoners in 2011." U.S. Department of Justice, Bureau of Justice Statistics. http://www.bjs.gov/content/pub/pdf/p11.pdf; Minton, Todd D. 2013. "Jail Inmates at Midyear 2012 – Statistical Tables." U.S. Department of Justice, Bureau of Justice Statistics. http://www.bjs.gov/content/pub/pdf/jim12st.pdf.

82 Neighly, Emsellem, and Christman (2014).

83 The Legal Action Center. *After Prison: Roadblocks to Reentry: A Report on State Legal Barriers Facing People with Criminal Records.* http:// www.lac.org/ roadblocks-to-reentry/ main.php?view=law&subaction=4.

84 Texas Occupations Code,Title 2, Chapter 53, SubchapterB, Sec. 53.025. http:// www. statutes.legis.state.tx.us/ Docs/ OC/htm/OC.53.htm.

85 Texas Department of Licensing and Regulation. "Guidelines for License Applicants with Criminal Convictions." http://www.tdlr.texas.gov/crimconvict.htm.

86 Hall, Matthew, Audrey Singer, Gordon F. De Jong, and Deborah Roempke Graefe. 2011. "The Geography of Immigrant Skills: Educational Profiles of Metropolitan Areas." *State of Metropolitan America* no. 33. The Brookings Institution. http:// www.brookings.edu/ ~/media/research/files/papers/2011/6/immigrants- singer/06_immigrants_singer.pdf.

87 Lopez, Fanny, Nancy Younan, and Rebecca Tancredi. 2014. "Foreign-Educated Engineers: Barriers to Employment and Professional Relicensing in Illinois." Illinois Coalition for Immigrant and Refugee Rights. http://icirr.org/content/report-discusses-barriers-immigrant-engineers-illinois.

88 Baker, Dean. 2014. "Doctors and Drugs: Promoting Growth and Equality through Free Trade." *Cato Online Forum.* http://www.cato.org/publications/cato-online-forum/doctors-drugs-promoting-growth-equality-through-free- trade.

89 Molloy, Raven, Christopher L. Smith, and Abigail Wozniak. 2014. "Declining Migration within the U.S.: The Role of the Labor Market." NBER Working Paper 20065.

90 Davis and Haltiwanger (2014).

91 Molloy, Raven, Christopher L. Smith, and Abigail Wozniak. 2011. "Internal Migration in the United States." *Journal of Economic Perspectives* 25, no. 3: 173-196. American Economic Association; Saks, Raven E. and Abigail Wozniak. 2011. "Labor Reallocation over the Business Cycle: New Evidence from Internal Migration." *Journal of Labor Economics* 29, no. 4: 697-739. The University of Chicago Press.

92 Shimberg and Roederer (1994) provide much of the framework that we discuss here. Shimberg, Benjamin and Doug Roederer. 1994. "Questions a Legislator Should Ask." Second Edition. Lexington, KY: The Council on Licensure, Enforcement and Regulation.

93 One concern with private certification in particular is that private competition could lead to a number of certifiers, leaving consumers unable to distinguish between high and low-quality certification. In response to this problem, the State could impose minimum standards or in some other way regulate private certification, or the State could itself shoulder the responsibility of certifying workers.

94 Gellhorn, Walter. 1976. "The Abuse of Occupational Licensing." *The University of Chicago Law Review* 44, no. 1: 6-27; Shimberg (1980).

95 Indiana General Assembly. 2015. House Bill 1303. https:// iga.in.gov /legislative/ 2015/ bills/ house/1303.

[96] American Physical Therapy Association. 2012. "APTA to Explore Feasibility of Transitioning PTA Education to Bachelor Degree Level." http:// www.apta.org/ PTinMotion/NewsNow/2012/6/15/HODRC20/.

[97] Hadfield (2014).

[98] Freed, Gary L., Kelly M. Dunham, and Acham Gebremariam. 2013. "Changes in Hospitals' Credentialing Requirements for Board Certification from 2005 to 2010." *Journal of Hospital Medicine* 8, no. 6: 298-303.

[99] Pew Health Professions Committee. 1995. "Reforming Health Care Workforce Regulation: Policy Considerations for the 21st Century." *Report of the Taskforce on Health Care Workforce Regulation*. http:// www.futurehealth.ucsf.edu/ Content/ 29/ 1995-12_ Reforming_Health_Care_Workforce_Regulation_Policy_Considerations_for_the_21st_Century.pdf.

[100] Swankin, LeBuhn, and Gulish (2010).

[101] Connecticut General Assembly. 2009. "Scope of Practice Determination for Health Care Professions." Legislative ProgramReview and Investigations Committee. http:// www. cga.ct.gov/2009/pridata/Studies/PDF/Scope_of_Practice_Final_Report.PDF.

[102] Connecticut Department of Public Health. 2015. *Scope of Practice Requests for 2014– 2015*. http:// www.ct.gov/ dph/cwp/view.asp?a=3121&Q=563950&PM=1.

[103] This paragraph benefited from a conversation with the National Employment Law Project.

[104] Craddock, Larry. 2008. "'Good Moral Character' as a Licensing Standard." *Journal of the National Association of Administrative Law Judiciary* 28, no. 2: 450-469; See Massachusetts Department of Health and Human Services for example of a state regulation in Massachusetts requiring good moral character. Massachusetts Department of Health and HumanServices. *Good Moral Character Requirements for Licensing*. http://www.mass.gov/eohhs/gov/departments/dph/programs/hcq/dhpl/nursing/licensing/good-moral-character- requirements-for-licensure.html.

[105] Neighly, Emsellem, and Christman (2014).

[106] The Council on Licensure, Enforcement, and Regulation defines sunset and sunrise reviews as follows: "Sunset is the automatic termination of regulatory boards and agencies unless legislative action is taken to reinstate them... Sunrise is a process under which an occupation or profession wishing to receive State certification or licensure must propose the components of the legislation, along with cost and benefit estimates of the proposed regulation. The profession must then convince the legislators that consumers will be unduly harmed if the proposed legislation is not adopted." Council on Licensure Enforcement and Regulation. *Sunrise, Sunset and State Agency Audits*. http://www.clearhq.org/page-486181.

[107] *Fla. Stat.* § 11.62

[108] Thornton and Timmons (2015).

[109] Maine Revised Statutes Title 32 § 60-J. http:// legislature.maine.gov/ statutes/ 32/ title 32 sec60-J.html; Maine Department of Professional and Financial Regulation. 2015. Private Correspondence.

[110] Loten, Angus and Sarah E. Needleman. 2014. "State Licensing Boards Under Fire from Within." *The Wall Street Journal*. http://www.wsj.com/articles/state-licensing-boards-under-fire-from-within-1409184515; Rhode, Deborah. 1981. "Policing the Professional Monopoly: A Constitutional and Empirical Analysis of Unauthorized Practice Prohibitions." *Stanford Law Review* 34, no. 1: 1-112.

[111] Kleiner (2015) includes a discussion of DORA.

[112] Colorado's Department of Regulatory Agencies. Interview by National Economic Council. 2015. Washington, DC.

[113] See http://www.michigan.gov/lara/0,4601,7-154-10573_11472-275935--RSS,00.html.

[114] Michigan Department of Licensing and Regulatory Affairs. 2012. *Office of Regulatory Reinvention Issues Recommendations to Deregulate 18 Occupations; Eliminate 9 Boards.*

http:// www.michigan.gov/ lara/ 0,4601,7-154-10573_11472-275935--RSS,00.html; Michigan Licensing and Regulatory Affairs. 2015. Private correspondence.

[115] Thornton and Timmons (2015); Texas Legislature. 2015. Senate Bill 202.

[116] North Carolina General Assembly Legislative Services Office. 2014. "Occupational Licensing Agencies Should Not be Centralized, but Stronger Oversight is Needed." *Final Report to the Joint Legislative Program Evaluation Oversight Committee* no. 2014-15. http://www.ncleg.net/PED/Reports/documents/OccLic/OccLic_Report.pdf.

[117] North Carolina General Assembly Legislative Services Office (2014).

[118] Swankin (2012); Shimberg (1980); Pew Health Professions Committee (1995).

[119] Shimberg (1980).

[120] Citizen Advocacy Center. 1995. *Public Representation on HealthCare Regulatory, Governing, and Oversight Bodies: Strategies for Success.*

[121] U.S. Department of Treasury and U.S. Department of Defense (2012).

[122] Executive Order 13563. January 18, 2011. Federal Register 76(14).

[123] Holen, Arlene. 1978. "The Economics of Dental Licensing." Department of Health, Education and Welfare.

[124] Kleiner, Morris M. and Robert T. Kudrle. 2000. "Does Regulation Affect Economic Outcomes? The Case of Dentistry." *Journal of Law and Economics* 43, no. 2: 547-582. The University of Chicago Press.

[125] Carpenter II, Dick M. 2012. "Testing the Utility of Licensing: Evidence from a Field Experiment on Occupational Regulation." *Journal of Applied Business and Economics* 13, no. 2: 28-41.

[126] Kleiner, Morris M. and Kyong Won Park. 2014. "Life, Limbs and Licensing: Occupational Regulation, Wages, and Workplace Safety of Electricians, 1992-2007." *Monthly Labor Review*. U.S. Bureau of Labor Statistics.

[127] Phelan, John J. 1974. "Economic Report [on the] Regulation of the Television Repair Industry in Louisiana and California: A Case Study: Staff Report to the Federal Trade Commission." 23. U.S. Government Printing Office.

[128] Fairman et al. (2011); Institute of Medicine (2010); Cassidy (2012).

[129] Stanik-Hutt et al. (2013).

[130] Klee, Mark A. 2013. "How Do Professional Licensing Regulations Affect Practitioners? New Evidence." U.S. Bureau of Labor Statistics, SEHSD Working Paper 2013-30.

[131] Morris M. Kleiner and Richard M. Todd. 2009. "Mortgage Broker Regulations that Matter: Analyzing Earnings, Employment, and Outcomes for Conusmers." *Studies of Labor Market Intermediation*, David H. Autor, ed.

[132] Kleiner, Morris. 2006. Licensing occupations: Enhancing quality or restricting competition? Kalamazoo, MI: Upjohn Institute.

[133] Maya N. Federman, David E. Harrington, and Kathy J. Krynski. 2006. "The Impact of State Licensing Regulations on Low-Skilled Immigrants: The Case of Vietnamese Manicurists." *American Economic Review*, 96(2): 237-241.

[134] Alison Cathles' David E. Harrington, and Kathy Krynski. 2010. "The Gender Gap in Funeral Directors: Burying Women with Ready-to-Embalm Laws?" *British Journal of Industrial Relations* 48(4).

[135] Kuo, Yong-Fang, et al. 2013. "States with the Least Restrictive Regulations Experienced the Largest Increase in Patients Seen By Nurse Practitioners." *Health Affairs* 32 (7): 1236-1243.

[136] Carroll, S. and Gaston, R. "Occupational Restrictions and the Quality of Service Received: Some Evidence." Southern Economic Journal 47(4) (1981): 959.

[137] DePasquale and Stange (2014).

[138] Kleiner, Morris and Kyoung Won Park. 2010. "Battles Among Licensed Occupations: Analyzing Government Regulations on Labor Market Outcomes for Dentists and Hygienists." *NBER Working Paper* # 16560.

[139] Mark A. Klee. 2013. "How Do Professional Licensing Regulations Affect Practitioners? New evidence"; Morris Kleiner and Alan Krueger. 2010. "The Prevalence and Effects of Occupational Licensing." *British Journal of Industrial Relations*, 48 (4).

[140] Robert J. Thornton and Edward J. Timmons. 2010. "The Licensing of Barbers in the USA." *British Journal of Industrial Relations*, 48(4): 740-757; Robert J.Thornton and Edward J. Timmons. 2013. "Licensing One of the World's Oldest Professions: Massage." *Journal of Law and Economics*, 56(2): 371-388.

[141] Morris Kleiner and Alan Krueger. 2010. "The Prevalence and Effects of Occupational Licensing." *British Journal of Industrial Relations*, 48 (4).

[142] Morris M. Kleiner and Alan B. Krueger. 2013. "Analyzing the Extent and Influence of Occupational Licensing on the Labor Market." *Journal of Labor Economics*, 31(2).

[143] Holderness, Richard A., Stephen G. Valker, and Stephen D. Butler. "State-By-State Guide to Architect, Engineer, and Contractor Licensing." Aspen Publishers Online, 1995.

[144] Gittleman, Klee, and Kleiner (2015).

[145] Gittleman and Kleiner (2013).

[146] Klee (2013).

[147] Estimates reflect controls for certification, detailed occupation, region, government employment, business ownership, union membership, years of education, work experience, gender, race, and ethnicity."

[148] U.S. Department of the Treasury and U.S. Department of Defense (2012).

[149] DePasquale, and Stange (2014).

[150] U.S. Department of Treasury and U.S. Department of Defense (2012).

[151] Pashigian, B. Peter. 1979. "Occupational Licensing and the Interstate Mobility of Professionals." *Journal of Law and Economics* 22, no. 1: 1-25; Holen (1965).

[152] Survey of Income and Program Participation, 2008 Panel; UST Calculations.

In: Occupational Licensing
Editor: Margie Castro
ISBN: 978-1-63484-340-9


*Chapter 2*

# SUPPORTING OUR MILITARY FAMILIES: BEST PRACTICES FOR STREAMLINING OCCUPATIONAL LICENSING ACROSS STATE LINES*

***U.S. Department of the Treasury and U.S. Department of Defense***

The President and his administration have taken the initiative to make the care and well-being of our nation's veterans, service members, and military families a priority across all agencies of the government. Last year, the President unveiled *Strengthening Our Military Families: Meeting America's Commitment* – a document that outlined the commitment of 16 separate agencies to 47 initiatives designed to improve the lives of military families. First Lady Michelle Obama and Dr. Jill Biden have also made it their personal priority to support our nation's veterans, service members, and military families through their Joining Forces initiative.

As a result of the President's advocacy, and in response to conversations that the First Lady and Dr. Biden have had with military spouses, the Departments of Treasury and Defense have co- authored this report to highlight the impact of state occupational licensing requirements on the careers of military spouses. The report shows that military spouses are especially

---

* This is an edited, reformatted and augmented version of a report issued by the Department of Defense, February 2012.

affected by state occupational licensing requirements. About 35 percent of military spouses work in professions that require state licenses or certification. They move across state lines far more frequently than the general population. These moves present administrative and financial challenges, as illustrated in a case study of nursing licensing requirements.

The report identifies best practices that states and licensing bodies can adopt through legislation, as well as current Department of Defense initiatives that address this issue.

We believe the best practices described in this report provide a baseline for further improvements, and hope it is a call to action to support our military spouses while still maintaining professional standards that ensure public safety. We are asking state governments, licensing boards, and professional associations to join us in finding more efficient ways for military spouses and other mobile professionals to fulfill these state and professional licensing and certification requirements.

Our military spouses support the well-being and safety of our nation, and we can best appreciate their sacrifices and unique challenges by adopting practices that lessen the burdens of their frequent moves.

They have a compelling need and we are suggesting tangible solutions.

All that is needed is the willingness to take action.

Dr. Janice Eberly
Assistant Secretary of the Treasury
for Economic Policy

Dr. Jo Ann Rooney
Acting Under Secretary of Defense
Personnel and Readiness

# EXECUTIVE SUMMARY

On January 24, 2011, President Obama, First Lady Michelle Obama, and Dr. Jill Biden presented *Strengthening Our Military Families: Meeting America's Commitment* – a document that responded to the Presidential Study Directive calling on all Cabinet Secretaries and other agency heads to find better ways to provide our military families with the support they deserve. The directive was initiated to establish a coordinated and comprehensive federal approach to supporting military families, and it contains nearly 50 commitments by federal agencies in pursuit of this goal.

State licensing and certification requirements are intended to ensure that practitioners meet a minimum level of competency. Because each state sets its own licensing requirements, these requirements often vary across state lines. Consequently, the lack of license portability – the ability to transfer an existing license to a new state with minimal application requirements – can impose significant administrative and financial burdens on licensed professionals when they move across state lines. Because military spouses hold occupational licenses and often move across state lines, the patchwork set of variable and frequently time-consuming licensing requirements across states disproportionately affect these families. The result is that too many military spouses looking for jobs that require licenses are stymied in their efforts.

A spouse's employment plays a key role in the financial and personal well-being of military families, and their job satisfaction is an important component of the retention of service members. Without adequate support for military spouses and their career objectives, the military could have trouble retaining service members.

The Department of the Treasury and the Department of Defense (DoD) have conducted an analysis to highlight the importance of state occupational licensing requirements in the lives of licensed military spouses. The report demonstrates that military spouses often work in occupations that require a license or certification and that they have a relatively high rate of interstate mobility compared to the general population. The report also examines a case study of nursing licensing requirements to illustrate the administrative and financial burdens that licensed military spouses face when they move across state lines, and highlights current DoD initiatives that address these licensing issues. Finally, the report identifies best practices that states and licensing bodies can adopt to help reduce barriers for military spouses moving across state lines.

This report finds that:

- Nearly 35 percent of military spouses in the labor force require licenses or certification for their profession.
- Military spouses are ten times more likely to have moved across state lines in the last year compared to their civilian counterparts.

**Percent of Adult Population that Moved Across State Lines in the Last Year**

In a 2008 Defense Manpower Data Center (DMDC) survey of military spouses, participants were asked what would have helped them with their employment search after their last military move. Nearly 40 percent of those respondents who had moved indicated that "easier state-to-state transfer of certification" would have helped them.

This report highlights best practices that states can pursue to help licensed military spouses. These best practices to help make licenses more portable come at little cost to states, but could make a meaningful difference in the lives of many military families. These best practices include:

- *Facilitating endorsement of a current license* from another jurisdiction as long as the requirements for licensure in that jurisdiction are substantially equivalent to those in the licensing state, and the applicant:
  - Has not committed any offenses that would be grounds for suspension or revocation of the license in the other jurisdiction, and is otherwise in good standing in that jurisdiction; and

  - Can demonstrate competency in the occupation through methods as determined by the Board, such as having completed continuing education units, having had sufficient recent experience (in a full or part time, paid or volunteer position), or by working under supervision for a prescribed period.
- Providing a temporary or provisional license allowing the military spouse to practice while fulfilling requirements needed to qualify for endorsement in the licensing state, or awaiting verification of documentation supporting an endorsement. Temporary licenses should require minimum documentation, such as proof of holding a current license in good standing and marriage to an active duty Service member who is assigned to the state.
- Expediting application procedures so that:
  - The director overseeing licensing within the state has authority to approve license applications for the boards; and/or
  - The individual licensing boards have authority to approve a license based simply on an affidavit from the applicant that the information provided on the application is true and that verifying documentation has been requested.

DoD, through the DoD-State Liaison Office (DSLO), has an on-going program to address key issues with state policymakers. This program, USA4 Military Families, covers 10 key issues, including occupational licensing and eligibility for unemployment compensation benefits. As of February 2012, thirteen states have introduced bills addressing the aforementioned best practices, and DSLO is working with these legislators. Although DoD continues to work on these issues on behalf of military spouses, more work remains to be done.

## INTRODUCTION

Military spouses not only play an enormous role in supporting our armed forces, but they also endure recurring absences of their service member spouse, frequent relocations, and extended periods of single-parenting and isolation from friends and family.[1] Research suggests that the effects of these challenging circumstances can be mitigated by employment. Unfortunately, military spouses earn less than their civilian counterparts and are less likely to be employed, on average.[2,3] A RAND study found that nearly two-thirds of military spouses felt that being a military spouse negatively affected their opportunity to work because of the "frequent and disruptive moves" associated with a military lifestyle.[4]

**CIVILIAN SPOUSES OF ACTIVE DUTY SERVICE MEMBERS**[v]

**Number:** 612,709

- Army: (40%)
- Navy: (24%)
- Marine Corps: (13%)
- Air Force: (24%)

**Gender:**

- Female: 95%
- Male: 5%

**Average age:** 32

Average years married: 7.8 years

**Race/Ethnicity:**

- Non-Hispanic White: 68%
- Non-Hispanic Black: 9%
- Hispanic: 12%

**Education:**

- No College: 16%
- Some College: 49%
- Bachelor's Degree: 25%
- Advanced Degree: 10%

**Employment:**

- Labor participation rate: 57%
- Unemployment rate: 26%

**Age of Children*:**

- Have children 5 & under: 54%
- Have children 6-12: 30%
- Have children 13-17: 15%

*72% have children

Research on military spouses finds that employment positively affects their general well-being – both directly and indirectly. Specifically, satisfaction with career development prospects has a direct and statistically significant effect on military spouses' well-being.[6] However, many military spouses are not satisfied with their career prospects. One military spouse said, "as time passes and I am unable to find work, my career dies and I feel like I have to abandon my personal and professional goals because my spouse is [the] military."[7] Although many military families depend on two incomes, they often face difficulties in career maintenance: "having to leave an excellent job behind, be unemployed for months, then underemployed...all of this affects our family's finances."[8]

Military spouse employment and the associated financial and personal well-being is also an important component of the retention of service members. More than half of all active duty military personnel are married, and 91 percent of employed military spouses indicated that they wanted to work and/or needed to work.[9] Research suggests that spouse dissatisfaction with the ability to pursue career objectives may hinder re-enlistment. Not only are military spouses highly influential regarding re-enlistment decisions, but more than two-thirds of married service members reported that their decision to re-enlist was largely or moderately affected by their spouses' career prospects.[10]

Complicated state occupational licensing requirements contribute to the difficulties that spouses of military personnel face in the workforce. State licensing and certification requirements are intended to ensure that practitioners meet a minimum level of competency and to help "protect the public from unqualified providers."[11,12] Because each state sets its own licensing requirements, these requirements often vary across state lines. Consequently, the lack of license portability – the ability to transfer an existing license to a new state with minimal requirements – can impose significant administrative and financial burdens on licensed professionals when they move across state lines. Because nearly 35 percent of military spouses work in licensed or certified professions and are 10 times as likely to move across state lines than their civilian counterparts, military spouses are more frequently affected by the lengthy background checks, exams, fees, and other burdens associated with the lack of licensing portability.

Military spouses have expressed their frustration with the lack of licensing portability.

According to a May 2010 survey of military spouses conducted by Blue Star Families, a military family support group, almost half of respondents felt that being a military spouse negatively affected their ability to pursue a career, while one in five respondents cited difficulties arising from the lack of licensing portability.[13] One military spouse said, "moving from one state to another, with different licensing requirements, has been a challenge. My career, while fairly portable, has still been difficult to maintain."[14] Another military spouse, a real estate broker, explained the challenges of transferring licenses when she and her husband moved across state lines:

> I was a real estate broker in North Carolina when I met my husband. When we [moved] to Texas, my license was no longer valid...In order to reinstate my license, I would have had to attend Texas real estate school and pay Texas licensure fees. The cost to get my license and restart my business would have been more than I could have earned in the 18 months we lived there before [moving] to Kentucky. In Kentucky, I would have had to do it all over again.[15]

Given the volunteer nature of our military, the sacrifices military families make for this country, and the importance of retaining these families to maintain the readiness of our military, ensuring that licensing procedures do not needlessly hinder military spouses is critically important.

The first section of this report uses the Current Population Survey to demonstrate that military spouses often work in occupations that require a license or certification and that they have a relatively high rate of interstate mobility compared to the general population. The second section illustrates the administrative and financial burdens that military spouses face when they move across state lines by examining a case study of nursing licensing requirements. Finally, the third section highlights current DoD initiatives that address these licensing issues and discusses best practices that states and licensing bodies can adopt to help reduce barriers for military spouses moving across state lines.

## Part 1: Licensing and Mobility

This section uses data from the Annual Social and Economic (ASEC) supplement of the Current Population Survey (CPS) to demonstrate that military spouses often work in state licensed occupations and that they have a relatively high rate of interstate mobility compared to the general population. The CPS is the basis for official government labor force statistics, including the unemployment rate.[16] While the CPS does not survey military barracks, the data do include civilian spouses of service members even if they live on-base in civilian housing.

We constructed a sample of approximately 2,800 spouses of active duty, Guard and Reserve service members, by combining CPS labor force data from 2007 through 2011. Table 1 presents summary statistics for our sample of military spouses. Due to data constraints, we exclude dual-military families (in which both spouses are enlisted) from the analysis. About 95 percent of military spouses in our sample are female, which is consistent with personnel data from DoD.[17]

**Table 1. Gender and Population Estimate *of Military Spouses***

| | Population estimate | Sample size | Percent of Total |
|---|---|---|---|
| Women | 670,280 | 2,609 | 94.2% |
| Men | 43,511 | 162 | 5.8% |

Notes: Annual averages based on pooled 2007 through 2011 data from the ASEC supplement of the CPS.

Table 2 presents labor force statistics for military spouses and civilian spouses. Data from the CPS show that the labor force participation rate for military spouses has been about 57 percent over the past five years, with an unemployment rate of 9.3 percent.

**Table 2. Labor Force Participation and Unemployment Rate of Military and Civilian Spouses**

| | Military Spouses | Civilian Spouses |
|---|---|---|
| Labor Force Participation Rate | 56.8% | 72.8% |
| Unemployment Rate | 9.3% | 4.9% |

Notes: Annual averages based on pooled 2007 through 2011 data from the ASEC supplement of the CPS. Civilian spouse statistics are weighted to be comparable with the gender distribution of military spouses. Data are restricted to respondents aged 18 to 45.

Table 3 presents educational attainment for military spouses and civilian spouses using CPS data. Almost 44 percent of military spouses have "some college" but not a four-year degree, compared to 28 percent of civilian spouses. "Some college" includes receiving a degree or certificate from a community college or other short-term training program. In our sample, 38 percent of civilian spouses have at least a bachelor's degree, compared to 31 percent of military spouses.

**Table 3. Educational Attainment of Military and Civilian Spouses**

| | Military Spouses | Civilian Spouses |
|---|---|---|
| Less than high school | 2.9% | 9.9% |
| High school diploma (or equiv.) | 22.7% | 24.9% |
| Some college | 43.4% | 27.8% |
| Bachelor's degree or higher | 31.0% | 37.3% |

Notes: Averages based on pooled 2007 through 2011 data from the ASEC supplement of the CPS. Civilian spouse statistics are weighted to be comparable with the gender distribution of military spouses. Data are restricted to respondents aged 18 to 45.

## Occupations of Military Spouses

Table 4 presents the top 20 occupations among our sample of military spouses. Teaching is the most common occupation among military spouses, followed by child care services, and nursing. While many of the common occupations among military spouses are not licensed, some of the most popular professions, including teaching and nursing, do require licensure.

In a 2008 Defense Manpower Data Center survey of active duty military spouses, participants were asked what would have helped them with their employment search after their last military move. Nearly 40 percent of those respondents who had moved indicated that "easier state-tostate transfer of certification" would have helped them. This is not surprising given that a third of the respondents had "recently been employed" in an occupation with potential licensure requirements, and nearly half of the respondents suggested that they were interested in pursuing careers in licensed fields.[18] These responses are consistent with our findings in the CPS, which suggest that nearly 35 percent of military spouses in the labor force require licenses or certification for their profession.[19]

**Table 4. Top 20 Occupations for Military Spouses in the Labor Force**

| Rank | Occupation | Percent of total |
|---|---|---|
| 1 | Teachers (Pre-Kindergarten - 12th Grade)** | 5.2 |
| 2 | Child care workers* | 3.9 |
| 3 | Registered nurses** | 3.7 |
| 4 | Retail salespersons | 3.6 |
| 5 | Secretaries and administrative assistants | 3.5 |
| 6 | Waiters and waitresses | 3.0 |
| 7 | Receptionists and information clerks | 2.8 |
| 8 | Cashiers | 2.8 |
| | First-line supervisors/managers of retail sales | 2.5 |
| 9 | workers | |
| 10 | Customer service representatives | 1.8 |
| 11 | First-line supervisors/managers of office and administrative support workers | 1.6 |
| 12 | Accountants and auditors** | 1.6 |
| 13 | Nursing, psychiatric, and home health aides* | 1.5 |
| 14 | Managers, all other | 1.3 |
| 15 | Tellers | 1.3 |
| 16 | Dental assistants* | 1.2 |
| 17 | Financial managers | 1.2 |
| 18 | Postsecondary teachers | 1.2 |
| 19 | Stock clerks and order fillers | 1.2 |
| 20 | Other teachers and instructors | 1.2 |
| Memo | | |
| Other categories | | 53.9 |

Notes: Annual averages based on pooled 2007 through 2011 data from the ASEC supplement of the CPS. Data include unemployed workers. Double asterisks (**) denote occupations that require licenses; single asterisk (*) denotes occupations that have certification.

## Military Spouse Mobility

The ASEC supplement also asks respondents if they moved in the past year. Military spouses are approximately ten times more likely to have moved across state lines in the last year compared to the total population.[20] Table 5 presents mobility rates for military spouses and for the total population. On average, 15 percent of military spouses reported moving across state lines in the twelve months before the CPS survey, compared to only 1.5 percent of all CPS respondents.

**Table 5. Annual Percent of Adult Population Who Moved Across State Lines**

| | Percent Moved |
|---|---|
| Military Spouse | 15.2 |
| Civilian Spouse | 1.1 |
| Single / Unmarried | 1.8 |
| Memo | |
| All households | 1.5 |

Notes: Annual averages based on pooled 2007 through 2011 data from the ASEC supplement of the CPS, but reflect relocation in the year before the survey. Those who moved from overseas locations are excluded from this table.[21]

Because military spouses frequently hold occupations that have licensing requirements and because they move across state lines much more than the general population, complicated licensing processes are disproportionately burdensome for them. The next section will examine state licensing requirements for nurses as a case study of the difficulties that military spouses face when transferring their license across state lines.

## Part 2: Nurse Licensing Case Study Registered Nursing License Portability

Nursing is among the most popular professions for military spouses, and registered nurses must meet licensure requirements in each of the states where they practice. Even though the nursing profession has standardized several aspects of its licensing procedures, transferring a license when moving remains a complicated process because of variability in state licensing requirements. These problems are not unique to the nursing profession, and many licensed professionals face similar challenges when attempting to transfer their license across state lines.

To illustrate the administrative and financial burdens that licensed military spouses face when they move across state lines, this section examines a case study of nursing licensing requirements. This section documents the process for obtaining a new nursing license in any state, lists the standardized aspects of moving a nursing license to another state, and demonstrates the variability in licensure requirements across state lines.

### *Initial Licensing Hurdles*

To obtain an initial license as a registered nurse (RN) in any state, applicants must satisfy a large set of requirements. According to the Bureau of Labor Statistics, a nursing student must complete either a bachelor's degree, an associate's degree, or receive a diploma from an approved nursing program.[22] After completing a degree from an accredited program, an applicant for a registered nursing license must take the National Council Licensure Examination for Registered Nurses (NCLEX-RN). This nationally recognized test is administered by the National Council of State Boards of Nursing (NCSBN) and "measures the competencies needed to perform safely and effectively as a newly licensed, entry-level nurse."[23, 24] Passing a background check is also a requirement for nursing licensure in all states.

### *Standardized Aspects of the Nursing "Licensure by Endorsement" Process*

In general, a nurse changing his or her state of permanent residence must apply to the new state's licensing board for "licensure by endorsement," which is the process of transferring an existing nursing license to a new state. This process includes the application for and receipt of a temporary license while the application for a permanent license is processed. While a nurse waits for a temporary license, he or she may be unable to practice. The Nurse Licensure Compact (NLC) and the NURSYS online database help to address this inflexibility and facilitate the license transferring process by providing elements of standardization.

The NCSBN created the NLC in 1997.[25] Twenty-four states are members of the NLC. If a nurse changes his or her permanent residence from one compact state to another, the compact allows the nurse to practice using the previous state's license for up to 30 days. A change in residence requires that the nurse obtain a temporary or permanent license in the new state of residence in order to practice there for longer than 30 days. The NLC website states that nurses transferring their licenses when moving across state lines must "apply for licensure by endorsement, pay any applicable fees, and complete a declaration of primary state of residency in the new home state, whereby a new multistate license is issued and the former license is inactivated."[26] In other words, the 30-day privilege granted by this compact is separate from the temporary and permanent licenses granted through licensure by endorsement with the state nursing board. The compact agreement fills the gap between the time when the nurse moves and when a temporary license can be issued by the receiving state's nursing board.

The "licensure by endorsement" process has many components. A major part of this process is the verification of licensure in the previous state of residence. To this end, the NCSBN created an online data clearinghouse called NURSYS. Forty-six state nursing boards participate in NURSYS for verification of previous RN licensure.[27] If a nurse needs license verification from a state that does not participate in NURSYS, he or she must contact the latter state's nursing board for a state-specific verification. There is a $30 fee for the use of the NURSYS system.[28]

Although the NLC and NURSYS provide some standardization to the licensure by endorsement process, they do not ensure straightforward license portability for nurses moving across state lines and do not eliminate many of the non-uniform aspects of the application process, which are discussed below.

***Variability Among States in the "Licensure by Endorsement" Process***

While states frequently employ "licensure by endorsement" in nursing licensure, many states have additional requirements. Some states require "current experience"; this requirement mandates that prospective state license holders hold a current license and have worked as a nurse for some period specified by the state licensure board. The "current license" requirement often presents a significant complication when the license holder moves back to the United States after living overseas, as many military spouses do.

To allow nurses to continue practicing while their application for permanent licensure by endorsement is being processed, many state nursing boards offer temporary licenses after a preliminary background and qualifications checks. A clean record is usually required for a temporary license to be issued.[29]

Table 6 lists the 10 states with the largest active duty military populations and illustrates the variability in state nursing board requirements regarding license portability. For example, the wait time for a temporary license varies from as little as ten days in Virginia and Texas to up to six weeks in California. The time period for which a temporary license is valid also varies, from 30 days in Virginia to six months in California, Kentucky and North

Carolina.[30] The waiting time for a permanent license is often not published by the state nursing board, but in most states an application expires if not completed within one year of the start date. Application fees also vary: among the 10 states examined, the fee ranged from $43 in Colorado to $200 in Texas.[31]

### *Other Factors*

There are other factors that both facilitate and slow the licensure by endorsement process. Some states offer automated procedures for submission of fingerprints, transcripts and fees, but others do not.[32] Variability exists in the state board requirements for nursing licenses as well. Some states automatically accept nursing degrees issued by a nationally approved program operated in another state, while others require that a nurse fulfill specific course requirements prior to licensure by endorsement.[33] There is also variation in state licensure requirements on training about time-varying issues such as infection control, abuse, privacy, and medical records.[34]

Although license portability for nurses is generally more straightforward than for other professions, nurses moving across state lines still have to go through a rigorous application process to practice nursing in another state. The variability of these processes and the associated need to continually relicense through examination poses difficulties for military spouses in licensed occupations. Other professions popular among military spouses, such as teaching, have even more complicated license portability requirements. One aspect of teacher licensing is discussed in Box 1, below.

**Box 1. Teacher Testing Requirements**

License portability in teaching is very complicated. There are several tiers of licensing in teaching, and course requirements vary widely based on the state and the subject being taught. Even the relatively standardized portions of teaching license requirements, such as the required Praxis II subject tests, have very different state standards. The table below demonstrates how the Praxis II cutoff scores vary among states.[35]

In addition to the variability in Praxis II cutoff scores, many states with large military populations have their own individual examinations. Re-taking exams due to inconsistent cutoff scores or additional state tests pose time-consuming and expensive barriers to license portability.

**Praxis II Passing Scores in States with Large Military Populations**

| | Mathematics | English Language, Literature, and Composition | Social Studies | Biology | Chemistry |
|---|---|---|---|---|---|
| Colorado | 156 | 162 | 150 | .. | .. |
| Hawaii | 136 | 164 | 154 | 151 | 154 |
| Kentucky | 125 | 160 | 151 | 146 | 147 |
| Virginia | 147 | 172 | 161 | 155 | 153 |
| Difference between the highest and lowest passing scores | 31 | 12 | 11 | 9 | 7 |

## Table 6. Requirements for Transferring Nursing Licenses to a New State

| State | Does the state participate in NLC and NURSYS? | Application fee? | NCLEX Standardized Test | Temporary license valid for: | Wait time for temporary license: | Degree from accredited nursing education program needed? | Need Current Experience for Endorsement? |
|---|---|---|---|---|---|---|---|
| California | No (accepts verification from NURSYS, but does not provide information through NURSYS) | $100 or $151, depending on which fingerprinting method chosen | Yes, or SBTPE | 6 months | 4-6 weeks | Yes | No |
| Colorado | Yes | $43 | Yes, or SBTPE | 4 months | -- | Yes | No |
| Florida | NURSYS only | $223 | Yes, or SBTPE | -- | -- | Yes | Requires that the applicant worked as a nurse for 2 of the past |

| State | Does the state participate in NLC and NURSYS? | Application fee? | NCLEX Standardized Test | Temporary license valid for: | Wait time for temporary license: | Degree from accredited nursing education program needed? | Need Current Experience for Endorsement? |
|---|---|---|---|---|---|---|---|
| | | | | | | | 3 years |
| Georgia | No (accepts verification from NURSYS, but does not provide information through NURSYS) | $60 | Yes, or SBTPE | Does not typically provide temporary licenses | -- | Yes | Requires that the applicant worked as a nurse for 3 months or 500 hours in the past 4 years |
| Hawaii | No (accepts verification from NURSYS, but does not provide information through NURSYS) | $135-$180 | Yes (minimum score: 1600), or SBTPE (minimum score: 350) | 3 months | -- | Yes | No |
| Kentucky | Yes | $169.25 | Yes, or SBTPE | 6 months | 2 weeks | Yes | No |
| North Carolina | Yes | $188 | Yes (minimum score: 1600), or SBTPE (minumum score: 350) | 6 months | 2 weeks | Yes | No |
| Texas | Yes | $200 | Yes, or SBTPE minimum score: 350) | 120 days | 10 days | Yes | Requires that the applicant worked as a nurse or passed the appropriate RN exam in the past 4 years |

**Table 6. (Continued)**

| State | Does the state participate in NLC and NURSYS? | Application fee? | NCLEX Standardized Test | Temporary license valid for: | Wait time for temporary license: | Degree from accredited nursing education program needed? | Need Current Experience for Endorsement? |
|---|---|---|---|---|---|---|---|
| Virginia | Yes | $190 | Yes, or SBTPE | 30 days (may be extended at discretion of the board) | 10 days | Yes | No |
| Washington | NURSYS only | $92 | Yes, or SBTPE | -- | -- | Yes | No |

Note: '--'indicates unavailable information. Source: Web sites of the listed state's Board of Nursing. Contact information for each State Board is posted on the web site of the National Council of State Boards of Nursing, under a link for Boards of Nursing. See www.ncsbn.org.

## Part 3. Best Practices and Department of Defense Initiatives Best Practices to Facilitate Licensure Portability

DoD has identified best practices that states could adopt to facilitate license portability. Although DoD initially focused on promoting specific national compacts and national certifications for two career areas (teachers and nurses), the Department has recently shifted to initiatives easing the overall licensing process in a state to affect a broader population of licensed military spouses. The Nurse Licensure Compact, described earlier in this report, which gives nurses a more streamlined approach to transferring a current license to a member state, provided DoD the key concepts (temporary licenses and endorsements) to use with states for expediting licensure in other occupations, particularly if the state boards adopt methods that can expedite the application and approval process.

### *Licensure by Endorsement*

DoD and independent studies have consistently found that "licensure by endorsement" significantly eases the process of transferring a license from one state to another. Standard "licensure through examination" requires the applicant to go through numerous state reviews in addition to passing national or state examinations and may include a supervised practicum or apprenticeship. Licensure by endorsement streamlines the application and state verification process for applicants with active out-of-state licenses, helping licensed military spouse professionals return to work more quickly. Obtaining a license by endorsement usually only requires that the license from the previous state is based on requirements similar to those in the receiving state, and without a disciplinary record. However, in some cases, applicants must also show they have recently worked in the occupation (such as two out of the past four years) as a way of demonstrating current experience or proficiency. This latter requirement can pose a problem for military spouses who have been unable to practice due to assignment overseas or in other locations. If a spouse does not meet these requirements, they will, at a minimum, have to undergo further scrutiny than the endorsement process generally requires, and in some cases, go through the full "licensure through examination" process.

In its efforts to promote a broad-based model for licensure by endorsement, DoD worked closely with the Colorado Department of Regulatory Agencies (DORA) and interested state legislators, who subsequently passed Colorado House Bill (HB) 1175 in 2010. The legislation requires the licensure through endorsement process be considered for all 77 occupations regulated by DORA and allows the Director of DORA, rather than the individual licensing boards, to determine what is required to demonstrate competency for endorsement. This eliminates delays in waiting for boards to convene. Moreover, the legislation allows for alternative demonstrations of current experience, where required, such as accepting continuing education as a substitute when there are gaps in employment. This last provision especially helps military spouses who have been at an overseas duty station for an extended period of time and unable to practice.

Two other states enacted legislation in 2011 facilitating licensure by endorsement, each with a somewhat different approach to accommodating the needs of military spouses:

- Arizona enacted Senate Bill (SB) 1458 in 2011, which allows a military spouse applicant to qualify for endorsement with one year of experience in most occupations. For those few that require more than one year, it allows the applicant to be licensed if supervised by a licensed professional.

- Texas SB 1733, enacted in 2011, is similar to Colorado HB 1175 in that it allows the board to establish alternatives to current experience for proof of occupational competency. The bill also allows military spouses who had been licensed in Texas to reinstate their license if it expired less than five years ago and they spent at least six months of that time out of the state.

### *Temporary or Provisional Licensing*

Temporary or provisional licensure is another way to ease state-to-state transitions for military spouses. Typically, these licenses are valid for anywhere between 3 and 12 months. To apply, the applicant usually has to provide proof of a current license, obtain a background check, and submit an application and fee. These licenses allow applicants to be employed while they fulfill all of the requirements for a permanent license, including examinations or endorsement, applications, and additional fees. Typically, temporary or provisional licenses are managed separately by each occupational area within a state, as is true for the Nurse Licensure Compact, discussed earlier in this report.

Colorado also provided DoD's first opportunity to gain support for temporary/provisional licensing for military spouses. In 2008, Colorado enacted HB 1162 which provides interim authorization to a military spouse with a current teaching license from another state to work within a school district for one year and allows the school district to provide an induction program which will help the military spouse obtain a professional educator license.

In 2010, DoD worked with state legislators in Florida to develop legislation supporting temporary licensure that encompasses multiple occupations. Florida HB 713 impacts commercial occupations, such as Veterinarians and Certified Public Accountants, providing the military spouse a six month temporary license as long as the spouse is married to an active member of the military assigned in Florida, has a current license, submits fingerprints for a background investigation, and pays a fee for the temporary license. Moreover, the bill allows military spouses to retain their Florida licenses if they move out of state for military reasons, and to practice without renewing the license upon return as part of a military move. Florida extended these provisions to healthcare occupations in 2011 with the enactment of HB 1319.

Four other states (Alaska, Kentucky, Missouri, and Tennessee) enacted legislation in 2011 to provide temporary/provisional licenses to military spouses, primarily using the Florida model. Notably, Kentucky HB 301 and

Tennessee HB 968 provide licensure by endorsement if the spouse is qualified and temporary licensure if the spouse must fulfill additional state requirements to obtain a license (by endorsement or examination).

***Expedited Application Processes***

Approximately half of the states use a regulatory agency, such as the Department of Regulatory Agencies, while the others regulate through individual occupational boards and do not have an umbrella agency to expedite the application process. Different approaches were required to streamline the process in these states.

Through internal agreements with individual licensing boards, the Colorado Director of DORA has the authority to expedite the endorsement process by interceding to approve applications that fulfill the boards' criteria. Two states which do not have structures analogous to that in Colorado found other ways to expedite the application process:

- Montana provided an innovative approach in HB 94 that allows boards to approve an application (for an endorsement or temporary license) based on an affidavit stating that the information provided is true and accurate and that the necessary documentation is forthcoming. Boards review the documentation upon receipt and can take disciplinary action if there are discrepancies.
- Utah HB 384 allows their occupational boards to approve the use of out-of-state licenses for "*the spouse of an individual serving in the armed forces of the United States while the individual is stationed within this state, provided:*
  - *I.* *the spouse holds a valid license to practice a regulated occupation or profession issued by any other state or jurisdiction recognized by the division; and*
  - II. *the license is current and the spouse is in good standing in the state of licensure.*"

While the Utah provision is the most inclusive and least intrusive for a military spouse, DoD will monitor its implementation to see if out-of-state licenses are accepted by employers as equal in quality to in-state licenses. In developing expedited approaches that save military spouses time and money, DoD does not want to make licensure easier for military spouses to achieve at the expense of degrading their perceived value in their profession.

The 2011 legislative activity is now the baseline for further developments in 2012. Legislators, regulators, and boards have been innovative and have shown an overall willingness to address the core concern that military spouses have only a short time in a location to establish their households, obtain new licenses, find employment within their professions, and progress in their skills and abilities. 2012 may provide additional innovation and opportunities to improve licensure portability for military spouses around the following integrated set of concepts:

- *Facilitating endorsement of a current license* from another jurisdiction as long as the requirements for licensure in that jurisdiction are substantially equivalent to those in the licensing state, and the applicant:
    - Has not committed any offenses that would be grounds for suspension or revocation of the license in the other jurisdiction, and is otherwise in good standing in that jurisdiction; and
    - Can demonstrate competency in the occupation through various methods as determined by the Board, such as having completed continuing education units, having had sufficient recent experience (in a full or part time, paid or volunteer position), or by working under supervision for a prescribed period.
- *Providing a temporary or provisional license* allowing the military spouse to practice while fulfilling requirements needed to qualify for endorsement in the licensing state, or awaiting verification of documentation supporting an endorsement. Temporary licenses should require minimum documentation, such as proof of holding a current license in good standing and marriage to an active duty Service member who is assigned to the state.
- *Expediting application procedures* so that:
    - I. The director overseeing licensing within the state has authority to approve license applications for the boards; and/or
    - II. The individual licensing boards have authority to approve a license based simply on an affidavit from the applicant that the information provided on the application is true and that verifying documentation has been requested.

# OTHER DEPARTMENT OF DEFENSE INITIATIVES

## DoD Military Spouse Discussion Board

Although these current licensure initiatives appear very promising, DoD is reaching out to military spouses for their input on how best to alleviate the hindrances created by licensure requirements. Spouses have been encouraged to share their stories and concerns about the licensure process and provide examples of real world solutions. DoD posted a discussion board on Facebook.com to facilitate the aggregation of these stories and issues.

DoD also recognizes that best practices developed thus far with states may not cover all occupations and all impediments. With the exception of legislation passed in Colorado in 2008 for teachers entering the state, DoD is not aware of changes improving licensure for military spouses in this particular profession. Similarly, the legislation recently passed has specifically excluded attorneys. DoD launched specific discussion board sessions to learn more about the processes for obtaining teaching or law licenses and the barriers faced in maintaining these licenses while moving with the military. To further this discussion, DoD has invited interested military spouses who are teachers and attorneys to join groups to continue this dialogue.

Spouses who are attorneys have responded through the Military Spouse JD Network (MSJDN), an organization established by military spouses to advocate for provisional bar membership, to educate the legal community about military spouses, and to build a network to support improved career opportunities. DoD is working with the JD Spouse Network to achieve accommodations for attorneys.

### *MyCareer Advancement Account (MyCAA) Program*

DoD currently operates the MyCAA program, which provides flexible, self-managed education and training accounts that enable military spouses of junior service members to gain the skills needed to successfully enter, navigate, and advance in portable careers. The accounts offer up to $4,000 to eligible spouses for pursuit of an Associate's degree, or license or credential leading to a portable career. Accounts are available to military spouses married to service members serving on active duty in the junior Enlisted, Warrant Officer and Officer grades.[36] Funds may be used by eligible military spouses entering the workforce or transitioning between jobs and careers, and to incumbent workers in need of new skills to remain employed or move up the career ladder. Accounts must be used to pay for expenses directly related to the attainment of an Associate's degree, license, or industry-recognized credential. The accounts have helped build the financial stability of military families. In FY11, approximately 38,000 spouses applied for and were provided MyCAA financial assistance.

### *Military Spouse Employment Partnership (MSEP)*

The Military Spouse Employment Partnership (MSEP) is a targeted recruitment and employment partnership solution that connects corporate partners with military spouses who are seeking fulfilling portable careers. MSEP supports spouses of members on active duty, in the National Guard, and Reserves from all Services. MSEP partners offer flexible job opportunities that can withstand relocations, deployments, and other aspects of military life that have made career advancement so difficult for spouses in the past. MSEP now has almost 100 vetted "Fortune 500 Plus" employers participating, with over 150,000 jobs posted to its web portal (www.MSEPJobs.com) and 10,000 spouses who have been hired. As an MSEP Partner, a company agrees to:

- Identify and promote career opportunities for military spouses;
- Post job openings and a corporate human resources employment page on the MSEP Web portal;
- Offer transferable, portable career opportunities to relocating military spouse employees;
- Mentor incoming MSEP corporate partners;
- Participate in an annual MSEP meeting; and
- Document and provide employment data on military spouses hired.

MSEP's goal is to level the playing field and help military spouses connect with companies that are searching for skilled employees. Moreover, the impact of MSEP goes beyond just reducing the unemployment rate for military spouses by connecting employers to a large and diverse body of exceptionally capable, dedicated, and motivated workers. MSEP provides meaningful career opportunities that are compatible with the spouse's military service, which supports families remaining in the military.

### *Unemployment Compensation Eligibility*

Military spouses face many challenges associated with frequent mobility, including the loss of income associated with the relocation process. In 2004, DoD began working with states to enable military spouses who become unemployed because of their service member's reassignment to be eligible for unemployment compensation. Prior to DoD's involvement in this issue, most state statutes and policies viewed a spouse leaving a job due to a military move as a "voluntary" separation despite the fact that their departures are involuntary. Thirty-nine states now provide military spouses eligibility for unemployment compensation when they leave employment because of a military move, nearly triple the number of states in 2004. Eighty-five percent of military spouses live in these 39 states (plus the District of Columbia). The states granting unemployment compensation eligibility to working spouses in transition provide a much-needed financial bridge for military families during mandatory moves and allow licensed spouses the cushion to obtain new credentials and seek employment in their new state.

## Part 4. Conclusion

Occupational licensing requirements place a significant and undue burden on military spouses, a population that makes great sacrifices for this country. Because many military spouses hold occupational licenses and often move across state lines, the patchwork set of variable and frequently time-consuming licensing requirements across states disproportionately affect these families.

A spouse's employment plays a key role in the financial and personal well-being of military families, and their job satisfaction is an important component of the retention of service members. Without adequate support for military spouses and their career objectives, the military could have trouble retaining service members.

Although further research will be conducted to pinpoint the most effective ways to help licensed military spouses when they transition across state lines, DoD has already identified several best practices that states can implement to ease job transitions for this population. These best practices — licensure by endorsement, temporary licensing, and expedited application processes — come at little cost to states, but would make an enormous difference in the lives of licensed military spouses.

DoD, through the DoD-State Liaison Office (DSLO), has an ongoing program to address key issues with state policymakers. This program, USA4 Military Families, covers 10 key issues, which include occupational licensing and eligibility for unemployment compensation benefits. As of February 2012, thirteen states have introduced bills addressing the aforementioned best practices, and DSLO is working with these legislators. This is encouraging and shows that states are willing to consider this valuable change. The Administration encourages all states to examine these best practice initiatives and work with DoD on their implementation. DoD will track the enactment of legislation to measure the change in processes and continue to request feedback from military spouses to ensure these processes meet their needs.

For additional information on these initiatives or to contact the DSLO, please visit www.usa4militaryfamilies.org and click on the licensure issue. Although DoD continues to work on these issues on behalf of military spouses, more work remains to be done.

## APPENDIX 1: LICENSING AND CERTIFICATION

There are two major types of occupational skill verification: certification and licensing. Certification is less stringent than licensing, and is meant to ensure that practitioners meet a minimum standard of knowledge about their field. Professions as varied as car mechanics and travel agents are certified. Licensing gives the practitioner a "right to practice," which differs from certification in that it is illegal to practice without a license.[37] Possessing a license indicates that the practitioner has satisfied government requirements by passing exams, completing education requirements, satisfying background checks, completing administrative paperwork, and paying fees.[38] A wide range of professions are licensed, including secondary school teachers, healthcare professionals (including nurses, doctors and medical technicians), lawyers, and social workers.

For most licensed professions, state boards administer the licensure process. Because of the variability in the licensing requirements from state to state, groups that are highly mobile and work largely in licensed fields frequently face administrative difficulties due to the lack of licensing portability.

## APPENDIX 2: TOP 20 STATES WITH THE MOST ACTIVE DUTY MILITARY SPOUSES

| State | Number of Military Spouses (total) | Military Spouses per 1000 Civilian Spouses |
|---|---|---|
| Hawaii | 25,875 | 119.7 |
| Alaska | 12,025 | 103.4 |

| State | Number of Military Spouses (total) | Military Spouses per 1000 Civilian Spouses |
|---|---|---|
| Virginia | 65,889 | 46.2 |
| North Carolina | 55,563 | 33.8 |
| Kentucky | 25,896 | 30.2 |
| Washington | 32,553 | 27.6 |
| Colorado | 23,292 | 27.1 |
| Kansas | 15,183 | 26.7 |
| Georgia | 38,563 | 24.9 |
| North Dakota | 3,030 | 22.1 |
| New Mexico | 6,309 | 18.5 |
| South Carolina | 13,730 | 17.5 |
| Texas | 66,936 | 16.8 |
| Oklahoma | 11,301 | 15.7 |
| Wyoming | 1,610 | 15.2 |
| Nevada | 5,387 | 14.4 |
| Maryland | 13,883 | 14.0 |
| California | 72,422 | 12.3 |
| Delaware | 1,819 | 11.9 |
| Louisiana | 9,423 | 11.6 |

Note: Location of spouses is based on the assignment of the service member. Service members stationed in the District of Columbia are omitted. Numbers are as of September 30, 2011.

## References and Notes

[1] In this report, "military spouses" refer to the civilian spouses of military personnel.

[2] Lim, Nelson, Daniela Golinelli, and Michelle Cho. "Working Around the Military" Revisited: Spouse Employment in the 2000 Census Data. Santa Monica, CA: RAND, 2007.

[3] Where the civilian population is adjusted for the gender composition of the military spouse population

[4] Lim, Nelson, Daniela Golinelli, and Michelle Cho. "Working Around the Military" Revisited: Spouse Employment in the 2000 Census Data. Santa Monica, CA: RAND, 2007.

[5] DMDC (2011). 2010 Military Family Life Project: Administration, datasets, and codebook (Report No. 2010-031). Arlington, VA: DMDC. All data are from 2010.

[6] Rosen, Leora N., Jeannette R. Ickovics, and Linda Z. Moghamdam. "Employment and Role Satisfaction." Psychology of Women Quarterly 14 (1990): 371-85

[7] Blue Star Families. "2010 Military Family Lifestyle Survey." Blue Star Families. 07 Jan. 2011.

[8] Blue Star Families. "2010 Military Family Lifestyle Survey." Blue Star Families. 07 Jan. 2011.

[9] Defense Manpower Data Center, 2008 DMDC Survey of Active Duty Spouses. Available: https://www.dmdc.osd.mil/appj/dwp/index.jsp

[10] Defense Manpower Data Center, 2008 DMDC Survey of Active Duty Spouses. Available: https://www.dmdc.osd.mil/appj/dwp/index.jsp

[11] See Appendix 1 for the difference between 'certification' and 'licensing.'

[12] Krueger, Alan B. "Do You Need a License to Earn a Living? You Might Be Surprised at the Answer." The New York Times. 02 Mar. 2006. Web. 07 Jan. 2011.

[13] Blue Star Families. "2010 Military Family Lifestyle Survey." Blue Star Families. 07 Jan. 2011. The Blue Star Families survey was an informal survey of military spouses.

[14] Blue Star Families. "2010 Military Family Lifestyle Survey." Blue Star Families. 07 Jan. 2011.

[15] Blue Star Families. "2010 Military Family Lifestyle Survey." Blue Star Families. 07 Jan. 2011.

[16] The CPS consists of a representative sample of about 60,000 households a month, and labor force questions are asked concerning all working-age adult members in the household. The ASEC CPS supplement includes detailed questions on the occupation of all working-age adults.

[17] Department of Defense Personnel Files; this does not include spouses who are themselves a part of the military.

[18] Defense Manpower Data Center, 2008 DMDC Survey of Active Duty Spouses.Available: https://www.dmdc.osd.mil/appj/dwp/index.jsp

[19] Using CPS and a list of licensed occupations from Kleiner, Morris M., and Alan B. Krueger." The Prevalence and Effects of Occupational Licensing." British Journal of Industrial Relations 48.4 (2010): 676-87.

[20] Excludes moves from overseas.

[21] These data are from 2006-2010 because questions regarding mobility are asked of the previous year. These data were compiled using pooled data from 2007 to the 2011 ASEC CPS supplement.

[22] "Registered Nurses." U.S. Bureau of Labor Statistics. 17 Dec. 2009. Web. 22 Jan. 2012.

[23] Before 1982, this test was called the State Board Test Pool Examination (SBTPE), and results from this older version of the test are still accepted by state nursing boards.

[24] National Council of State Boards of Nursing. "What Is NCLEX?" Web. 22 Jan. 2012.

[25] Broun, Caroline N. "About NCLA." Nurse Licensure Compact Administrators. 2010. Web. 07 Jan. 2011.

[26] National Council of State Boards of Nursing. "Nurse Licensure Compact: Fact Sheet for Licensees and Nursing Students." NCLA.

[27] National Council of State Boards of Nursing. "NURSYS." Nursys.com. 2011.Web. 22 Jan. 2012.

[28] National Council of State Boards of Nursing. "Frequently Asked Questions." NURSYS, 2011. Web. 7 Jan. 2011.

[29] Prior convictions and disciplinary actions are often reviewed by state boards on a case-by-case basis, taking into account the severity of prior offenses and any remediary activities that may have been required. Telephone conversation with Danny Cope, California Department of Consumer Affairs Board of Registered Nursing call center operator, October 20, 2010.

[30] Web sites of the listed state's Board of Nursing. Contact information for each State Board is posted on the web site of the National Council of State Boards of Nursing, under a link for Boards of Nursing. See www.ncsbn.org.

[31] Web sites of the listed state's Board of Nursing. See www.ncsbn.org.

[32] Telephone conversation with Danny Cope, California Department of Consumer Affairs Board of Registered Nursing call center operator, October 20, 2010.

[33] Telephone conversation with Diane Tompkins, Assistant Director of Certifications, American Nurses' Credentials Center, October 21, 2010.

[34] Email correspondence with Anne Tumbarello, Director of the BSN Program at Mount St. Mary's College in Los Angeles, California.

[35] Educational Testing Service. "The Praxis Series Passing Scores by Test and State." Ets.org. 2010. Web. 12 Feb. 2012. The table lists four of the ten states with the largest active duty military populations for which Praxis cut off scores are available.

[36] Eligible military spouses include those who are married to Service members on active duty and those who are married to members of the Guard and Reserve who are on Federal orders. The junior grades covered are Enlisted grades E1 – E5, Warrant Officer grades W1 and W2, and Officer grades O1 and O2.

[37] Kleiner, Morris M., and Alan B. Krueger."The Prevalence and Effects of Occupational Licensing." British Journal of Industrial Relations 48.4 (2010): 676-87.

[38] Kleiner, Morris M., and Alan B. Krueger. "The Prevalence and Effects of Occupational Licensing." British Journal of Industrial Relations 48.4 (2010): 676-87.

# INDEX

## D



## E

## J



## L



## M



## N



## O



## P

## Q



## R



## S

## T



## U



## V



## W



## X